CAMBRIDGE

Brighter Thinking

# The English Revolution, 1625–1660

## A/AS Level History for AQA
## Student Book

Tom Wheeley

*Series Editors: Michael Fordham and David Smith*

# CAMBRIDGE
## UNIVERSITY PRESS

For my parents

University Printing House, Cambridge CB2 8BS, United Kingdom

Cambridge University Press is part of the University of Cambridge.

It furthers the University's mission by disseminating knowledge in the pursuit of
education, learning and research at the highest international levels of excellence.

www.cambridge.org
Information on this title: www.cambridge.org/ukschools/9781107573024 (Paperback)
www.cambridge.org/ukschools/9781107573055 (Cambridge Elevate-enhanced Edition)

First published 2015

*A catalogue record for this publication is available from the British Library*

ISBN 978-1-107-57302-4 Paperback
ISBN 978-1-107-57305-5 Cambridge Elevate-enhanced Edition
Additional resources for this publication at www.cambridge.org/ukschools

Cambridge University Press has no responsibility for the persistence or
accuracy of URLs for external or third-party internet websites referred to
in this publication, and does not guarantee that any content on such
websites is, or will remain, accurate or appropriate. Information regarding
prices, travel timetables, and other factual information given in this work
is correct at the time of first printing but Cambridge University Press
does not guarantee the accuracy of such information thereafter.

## Message from AQA

This textbook has been approved by AQA for use with our qualification. This means that we have checked that it broadly covers the specification and we are satisfied with the overall quality. Full details of our approval process can be found on our website.

We approve textbooks because we know how important it is for teachers and students to have the right resources to support their teaching and learning. However, the publisher is ultimately responsible for the editorial control and quality of this book.

Please note that when teaching the A/AS Level History (7041, 7042) course, you must refer to AQA's specification as your definitive source of information. While this book has been written to match the specification, it cannot provide complete coverage of every aspect of the course.

A wide range of other useful resources can be found on the relevant subject pages of our website: www.aqa.org.uk

# Contents

# About this Series

Cambridge A/AS Level History for AQA is an exciting new series designed to support students in their journey from GCSE to A Level and then on to possible further historical study. The books provide the knowledge, concepts and skills needed for the two-year AQA History A Level course, but it's our intention as series editors that students recognise that their A Level exams are just one step to a potential lifelong relationship with the discipline of history. This book has further readings, extracts from historians' works and links to wider questions and ideas that go beyond the scope of an A Level course. With this series, we have sought to ensure not only that the students are well prepared for their examinations, but also that they gain access to a wider debate that characterises historical study.

The series is designed to provide clear and effective support for students as they make the adjustment from GCSE to A Level, and also for teachers, especially those who are not familiar with teaching a two-year linear course. The student books cover the AQA specifications for both A/AS Level. They are intended to appeal to the broadest range of students, and they offer challenges to stretch the top end and additional support for those who need it. Every author in this series is an experienced historian or history teacher, and all have great skill in conveying narratives to readers and asking the kinds of questions that pull those narratives apart.

In addition to high-quality prose, this series also makes extensive use of textual primary sources, maps, diagrams and images, and offers a wide range of activities to encourage students to address historical questions of cause, consequence, change and continuity. Throughout the books there are opportunities to criticise the interpretations of other historians, and to use those interpretations in the construction of students' own accounts of the past. The series aims to ease the transition for those students who move on from A Level to undergraduate study, and the books are written in an engaging style that will encourage those who want to explore the subject further.

Icons used within this book include:

Key terms

Speak like a historian

Voices from the past/Hidden voices

Practice essay questions

Chapter summary

## About Cambridge Elevate

Cambridge Elevate is the platform which hosts a digital version of this Student Book. If you have access to this digital version you can annotate different parts of the book, send and receive messages to and from your teacher and insert weblinks, among other things.

We hope that you enjoy your AS or A Level History course, as well as this book, and wish you well for the journey ahead.

Michael Fordham and David L Smith
Series editors

# Introduction

Charles I was never meant to be king. He was the second son of James VI of Scotland and I of England: it was Charles's older brother, Henry, Prince of Wales, who was destined to be king. Thus, it was a quirk of fate that in 1612, Charles found himself thrust into the limelight by the untimely death of his brother. In the years that were to follow, Charles I would see his relations with Parliament sour and his kingdoms plunged into bloody civil war, while he himself would face the executioner's block.

When Charles succeeded to the throne in 1625, however, few people in England would have foreseen such political, social and economic calamity. For the most part, the English and the Scots were well suited to monarchy. As a form of government it seemed natural – just as a body is governed by its head, the same was deemed true of a nation. This natural obedience to the monarch was reinforced by the popular belief that a monarch received the right to govern from God alone: the Divine Right of Kings. In return for the people's loyalty the sovereign made a holy coronation oath to uphold the laws and customs of the people.

Yet, the English monarchy was not without its problems. When James VI and I had inherited the English throne from the last Tudor monarch, Elizabeth I, he also inherited a financial system that provided barely enough revenue to fund the kingdom in times of peace, let alone war. By 1625, the system remained unreformed, and the extravagance of his father led many of Charles's subjects to become critical of royal expenditure.

Those who were most critical were the members of Parliament (MPs) who sat in the House of Commons. It was these men, elected by the land-owning gentry of the kingdom, who decided on the subsidies, or taxes, that the king could raise from his subjects. In conjunction with their social superiors in the House of Lords, these men formed the king's Parliament, and sat whenever he needed advice, support for new laws or money. When they had served their purpose, it was the king's prerogative to dissolve them. Unlike modern Britain, where the monarch's government is drawn from democratically elected politicians, Charles I had the ability to choose his own ministers and advisors. As the chapters of this book will demonstrate, power over these rights of taxation and the appointment of ministers would continue to plague the rulers of Britain for decades to come. However, these issues were combined with another central issue: that of religion.

Nearly a century earlier Henry VIII had broken from the Roman Catholic Church, and so ended all allegiance to the Pope in Rome. This English Reformation of the Church echoed a broader European Reformation, in which Christians began to divide between Catholics and Protestants. Henry's split from Rome had seen him declare himself Head of the Church of England and despite an attempt by his daughter, Queen Mary, to reverse the process, Henry's Reformation (continued by his son Edward) had set England on a path to becoming one of the leading Protestant nations of Europe. Indeed, Charles's predecessors had fought hard to defend the Protestant cause – Elizabeth had confronted the might of Spain and defeated the Spanish Armada in 1588 while Charles's father, James VI and I, had finally gone to war in 1624 to defend Protestant allies in Europe against the forces of Catholicism.

Against this backdrop Charles I took the throne in 1625. It is hard to exaggerate how much people feared for the safety of the Protestant Reformation. The experience of war with Spain and various Catholic plots had done much to create a siege mentality among English and Scottish Protestants. The King was Defender of the Faith, and people expected him to safeguard Protestantism against all the horrors of the Roman Catholic Church. As if this wasn't enough, there had emerged in the previous decades, a 'hotter' sort of Protestant – Puritans, who felt that the English Reformation had not gone far enough, and that the last remnants of the old Catholic Church, its organisation and rituals, needed to be banished from the Church of England.

In time, the combined pressures of finance, unresolved questions over royal and parliamentary powers, and the central issue of religion and the future of England's Church would serve to bring the monarchy to its knees. In the upheaval of civil war new radical forces would be born – religious, social and political – and these forces would shape what has since been termed the English Revolution. Following the public execution of its king, England would experiment with republicanism before another man took the reins of power: Oliver Cromwell. Cromwell was destined to achieve great military success on the battlefield and, driven by his belief that God sought great things for the English, he would lead the nation into a period of unprecedented change and political experimentation.

Yet for all its upheaval, bloodshed and sacrifice, England's revolution saw it return to familiar forms of government and in 1660 it was Charles I's son, Charles II, who ruled. However, the scars left by the English Revolution ran deep and although the bodies of those men who killed the King in 1649 were strung up as a warning, the nation had been changed forever. The power of monarchs had been challenged, the role of Parliament had been asserted and a love of civilian rather than military rule had been fostered. In time, it would be this revolution that formed the foundation stone of future political and religious change in Britain.

## How to use this book

This book is intended to provide a chronological account of the main events of this period. At the same time it highlights key themes, such as political, financial and religious issues. The chapters will provide evidence that helps explain the causes of important events. In drawing on a range of sources the text attempts to achieve a degree of impartial objectivity. However, it should be remembered that this book is itself an example of historical interpretation, and it will be necessary for readers to use the information provided to reach their own conclusions.

The main narrative is supplemented with regular extracts from contemporary historical documents (primary evidence) as well historians' views (secondary sources). It is hoped that readers will use the activities and prompts for discussion to further their thinking on the issues presented. Above all, readers should look to apply the knowledge they gain from the chapters to think critically about the value of the source material presented and how far it gives a fair or representative view of an issue.

# 1 The emergence of conflict and the end of consensus, 1625–1629

In this section we will examine the early reign of Charles I and his approach to governing his kingdoms. We will look into:

- The legacy of James VI and I: religious issues and divisions; relations between Crown and Parliament; relations with foreign powers.
- Monarchy and Divine Right: the character and aims of Charles I; the Queen and the court; the King's advisors; ideas of royal authority.
- Challenges to the arbitrary government of Charles I: reactions against financial policies; conflict over the Church; reactions against foreign policy and the role of Buckingham.
- Parliamentary radicalism: personalities and policies of parliamentary opposition to the King; the Petition of Right; the dissolution of Parliament and the King's commitment to Personal Rule.

## The legacy of James VI and I

Ever since the reign of Henry VIII, England, along with the rest of Europe, had suffered from the split in the Christian faith. On the one hand the Catholics, or Papists as they were often known, remained loyal to the Pope in Rome. On the other hand the Protestants 'protested' at the abuses, rituals and ceremonies of the old Catholic Church and saw the Pope as the devil incarnate. This split, and the creation of the Protestant faith, was known as the **Reformation**, and under Henry VIII and his son Edward VI, England had emerged as a Protestant nation.

### Key term

**Reformation:** refers to the break in the Catholic Church whereby Protestants rejected the authority of the Pope in Rome and Catholic forms of worship and Church organisation. The Reformation split Europe. In England the Reformation took hold when Henry VIII broke from Rome and declared himself Supreme Governor of the Church of England.

3

Timeline

| 1625 | **January:** Mansfield's expedition<br>**27 March:** death of James VI and I; accession of Charles I<br>**3 May:** Charles marries Henrietta Maria of France<br>**18 June–11 July:** first session of Charles's first Parliament debates tonnage and poundage; Montagu attacked for Arminian views<br>**July:** Charles appoints Montagu as Royal Chaplain<br>**1–12 August:** second session of Charles's first Parliament<br>**September–November:** Buckingham's unsuccessful expedition to Cadiz |
|---|---|
| 1626 | **6 February–15 June:** Charles's second Parliament; attempted impeachment of Buckingham<br>**11–17 February:** York House Conference<br>**20 June:** Laud nominated as Bishop of Bath and Wells<br>**September:** Charles orders collection of Forced Loan |
| 1627 | **January:** England declares war on France<br>**June:** Buckingham leads army to Île de Ré off La Rochelle; assault fails<br>**November:** Five knights case |
| 1628 | **17 March–26 June:** First session of Charles's third Parliament: Petition of Right<br>**4 July:** Laud made Bishop of London<br>**5 July:** Richard Montagu made Bishop of Chichester<br>**July:** Confiscation of goods of London merchants, including John Rolle, who refused to pay tonnage and poundage<br>**23 August:** Buckingham assassinated<br>**15 December:** Wentworth made President of the Council of the North |
| 1629 | **20 January–10 March:** Second session of Charles's third Parliament<br>**2 March:** Three Resolutions<br>**27 March:** Charles issues proclamation stating that he will not recall Parliament until 'our people shall see more clearly into our intents and actions' |

## Religious issues and divisions

Catholics and Protestants differed in a number of ways. One area was in doctrine – the set of beliefs that defined their religious views. A key difference concerned salvation of the soul. While Catholics believed that the soul could be saved through faith, good works and prayer, Protestants believed that ascent to heaven was determined by predestination. This belief suggested that God had already decided the destination of people's souls. Those who were predestined to enter heaven were known as the Elect and could be identified by their godly lifestyle and devotion. This belief in predestination originated in the teachings of John Calvin, a mid-16th-century theologian who gave his name to a major branch of Protestant believers – Calvinists. Calvinism and its belief in predestination clashed with the Catholic belief that sinners could be absolved of, or forgiven, their sins.

Another area of disagreement centred round the fact that Catholics believed that during the ceremony of Holy Communion (or Eucharist) the bread and wine that represented the body and blood of Christ would be literally transformed into those substances (transubstantiation), whereas in the Protestant service the bread and wine served only as symbolic reminders of Christ's sacrifice. Thus, for Catholics, the ceremony of the Mass conducted before the high altar at the east end (the holiest part) of the church was of the utmost significance, as the priest was miraculously bringing about the physical presence of Christ. To Protestants this seemed mystical nonsense.

There were also practical differences. In Catholicism, Latin was the language used in services and the Bible. Only the educated would be able to understand and thus the learning of prayers by heart and the theatre of the ceremony were important features of Catholic belief. This was reinforced by ornate decoration of the church itself, with colourful depictions of biblical scenes from which the congregation could learn. The priest, as the intermediary between the people and God, was of vital importance and he conducted the Mass facing the high altar, dressed in ornate vestments (gowns) with his back to the congregation. Making the sign of the cross was a key feature of Catholic worship, as was bowing at the name of Christ and the worship of the saints.

In contrast, Protestants translated the Bible into English, believing that it was important that everybody was able to understand its teachings. In place of elaborate ceremony, a Protestant service was much simpler and would centre around a sermon (a speech inspired by an extract from the Bible). In order to allow people to focus on the 'word of God', the Church was decorated in plain style, often whitewashed. The priest, wearing plain vestments, would conduct the Holy Communion service from the centre of the church where the communion table was used instead of a high altar. This meant that the symbolic delivery of the bread and wine took place in the heart of the assembled congregation. In further rejection of the Catholic focus on ceremony, Protestants also abandoned practices such as the making of the sign of the cross and bowing at the name of Christ.

The **Dissolution** of the Catholic Church in England had seen Catholic worship suppressed, monasteries and nunneries forcibly closed, and all Church property taken by the Crown. Splits remained, however, and while the majority of the population embraced the new Protestant Church of England (and were known as Anglicans) there were some who retained their Catholic faith. At the other end of the religious spectrum there were the extreme Protestants who disliked any feature of the old Catholic forms of worship – these were the Puritans. Elizabeth I dealt with these divisions in a very sensible manner, creating what became known as the **Elizabethan Settlement**. Elizabeth had claimed that she 'did not wish to make windows into men's souls' but would be satisfied with outward conformity to Anglican worship. As long as her subjects attended Church of England services, their private beliefs remained their own. In effect this created a broad, all-encompassing state Church, even extending to those who remained privately Catholic but conformed outwardly to Anglican worship. Only if they failed to attend Anglican services did they suffer **recusancy fines**. The Elizabethan Settlement, albeit Protestant, made some important compromises that pleased those who were unhappy with the break from Rome. In particular, the monarch was termed 'governor' rather than 'head' of the Church of England and the system of bishops was retained to manage the Church. Some congregations continued to use greater degrees of ceremonial in services. Although the deeper theology surrounding transubstantiation and predestination remained an area for disagreement, the Settlement did much to paper over the cracks and create a working compromise.

When Elizabeth died in 1603, the Protestant king of Scotland, James VI, became James I of England and 'King of Great Britain', thus uniting the two kingdoms. In order to maintain national unity, James largely retained the Elizabethan Settlement. Thus, when Charles I became king in 1625, upon the death of his father, he inherited a broad national Church encompassing a range of religious groups.

That said, tensions had begun to emerge. The Gunpowder Plot of 1605, when a group of English Catholics sought to blow up James VI and I and his Parliament, did much to increase the pressures placed on Catholics. More importantly it raised fears and embedded the idea of a grand Catholic conspiracy in the English popular imagination.

---

**Key term**

**Dissolution:** the ending of a parliament. Legally, the right of dissolution lay with the monarch

**Key term**

**recusancy fines:** fines aimed at Catholics who failed to conform to Church of England services.

**Key term**

The **Elizabethan Settlement:** established to end a period of religious conflict between Catholics and Protestants in England. It was brought about by two acts of 1559. First, the Act of Supremacy asserted that the Church of England, under the supreme governorship of the monarch, was independent of the Pope in Rome. Second, the Act of Uniformity imposed a Book of Common Prayer and set down rules for services and the decoration of churches.

CONCILIVM SEPTEM NOBILIVM ANGLORVM CONIVRANTIVM IN NECEM IACOBI ·I· MAGNÆ BRITANNIÆ REGIS TOTIVSQ ANGLICI CONVOCATIPARLEMENTI.

**Figure 1.1:** An engraving showing the Catholic conspirators responsible for the Gunpowder Plot in 1605. The idea of a Catholic conspiracy haunted the minds of English Protestants.

The common belief was that the Catholics sought to bring down Protestantism in Europe and with it the English Church and the English political system that defended the 'true' religion. This fear of Catholicism dominated English political and religious thought for decades. Another source of religious tension came from the Puritans and their attempts to end elements of Catholic-style worship that had remained in Anglican services. James had pleased many Puritans by compromising on some of their demands and had commissioned the famous King James Bible (retranslating the Bible into English). However, one major area of contention remained – the existence of bishops. The hierarchical system of archbishops and bishops (the episcopacy) ensured the king was in control of the clergy who conducted the weekly services throughout the kingdom. However, while the episcopal system meant worship remained uniform, the Puritans disliked it. To them it was too controlling and too similar to the hierarchy of the old Catholic Church; they wanted freedom to preach and run services in their own way. Another group that disliked the episcopal system was the Presbyterian Scots. By the time of Charles's accession to the throne his father had managed to get the Scots to accept bishops into the Scottish Kirk; however, the Kirk remained fiercely separate from the Church of England. The Presbyterian system of worship gave great independence to parish priests and congregations to run services as they saw fit.

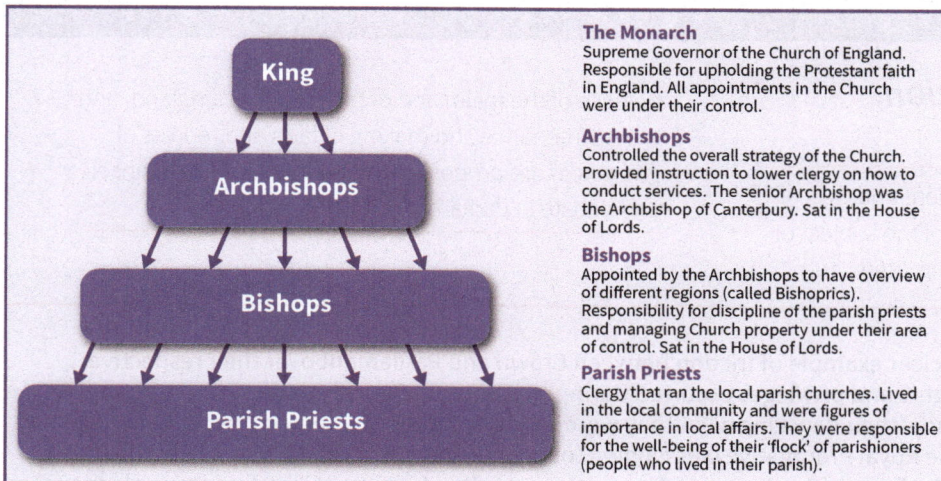

**The Monarch**
Supreme Governor of the Church of England. Responsible for upholding the Protestant faith in England. All appointments in the Church were under their control.

**Archbishops**
Controlled the overall strategy of the Church. Provided instruction to lower clergy on how to conduct services. The senior Archbishop was the Archbishop of Canterbury. Sat in the House of Lords.

**Bishops**
Appointed by the Archbishops to have overview of different regions (called Bishoprics). Responsibility for discipline of the parish priests and managing Church property under their area of control. Sat in the House of Lords.

**Parish Priests**
Clergy that ran the local parish churches. Lived in the local community and were figures of importance in local affairs. They were responsible for the well-being of their 'flock' of parishioners (people who lived in their parish).

**Figure 1.2:** The episcopal system of the Church of England.

## Relations between Crown and Parliament

The original purpose of English Parliaments was to provide money to the monarch. The monarch could call a Parliament whenever he or she wished in order to vote subsidies (the right to raise, or levy, a tax). Members of Parliament (MPs) often went beyond this remit and discussed areas of national importance upon which the monarch had the right to decide. These areas were known as the **Royal Prerogative** and included religious and foreign policy. Discussion of these issues by MPs had been a constant source of friction between monarchs and their Parliaments for decades, but by the time Charles became king, Parliaments had often been allowed to discuss them in the hope that they would more readily vote the Crown the subsidies it needed. During the reign of Elizabeth I, for example, Parliaments had regularly used the monarch's financial needs as an excuse to discuss issues concerning the Royal Prerogative, such as the conduct of the war, religious policy, and economic policies like the selling of monopolies (see Figure 1.6). This was not so much a long-term attempt to challenge the power of the monarch's prerogatives, but rather MPs seizing the opportunity to discuss matters of concern as they arose. By 1610 an attempt to provide James VI and I with a regular income of £200 000 (called The Great Contract) had failed, one reason being that MPs feared it would give the monarch too much freedom to act without calling a parliament. In short, Parliament was willing to use finances as a bargaining tool on issues that were strictly speaking the remit of the monarch.

By 1625, Parliament had developed a strong sense of its own rights, emboldened by certain parliamentary privileges. These included elections that were free from royal interference and freedom of speech on matters that affected the 'commonwealth' (the good of the nation). This freedom was reinforced by the convention that the monarch would not enter the House of Commons and that MPs were immune from arrest while Parliament was in session. Nonetheless, they too had to tread a fine line, and if they spoke out too forcefully, the monarch could exercise the right to dissolve Parliament at will. Indeed, there was no explicit rule that said how often, or for how long, parliaments should sit. It was only the need to be granted taxes that ensured regular parliaments were called. By the beginning of the 17th century it was clear that certain grey areas existed, such as the status of MPs who were accused of treason and Parliament's willingness to use **impeachment** as a means to hold ministers of the Crown to account.

> **Key term**
>
> **Royal Prerogative:** a set of powers exercised by the monarch or his ministers. These included control of religious and foreign policy, and the declaration of war and peace.

> **Key term**
>
> **impeachment:** the formal legal process operated by Parliament by which an official, such as an MP, lord or minister of the Crown can be accused of illegal acts and removed from post.

## Voices from the past

### The Commons' Protestation, 18 December 1621

The liberties of Parliament are the ancient and undoubted birthright and inheritance of the subject of England; and affairs concerning the King, State, and defence of the realm and of the Church of England, and the maintenance and making of laws and redress of grievances are proper subjects and matters of counsel and debate in Parliament. [2]

## Key terms

**ancient constitution:** the term used to describe the balance that was thought to exist between the three main elements of the political system – the Crown, the Lord and the Commons. England was thought to have evolved a finely balanced constitution that ensured that no one element was too powerful. This balance of power was seen as something sacred that should be preserved at all costs.

**Common Law:** developed over time by the rulings of judges on particular cases. These rulings set precedents that then bind decisions in future legal cases, thus providing continuity and equality of justice.

The **Thirty Years' War** (1618–48): a religious war in Europe fought between Protestant and Catholic states. Although England had been at peace in the 1630s, some Englishmen gained valuable military experience in this conflict fighting as hired mercenaries. The only other military experience was derived from the unsuccessful military operations in which England became embroiled in the 1620s.

A clear example of friction between Crown and Parliament over their respective rights and privileges occurred during James's first Parliament in 1604. Eager to show their new king what they were made of, 72 MPs expressed their concern that the Royal Prerogative was gaining too much strength. Their complaint, entitled 'The Form of Apology and Satisfaction', resulted from royal interference in elections in Buckinghamshire. In it they complained that 'The Prerogatives of princes may easily and do daily grow, [yet] the privileges of the subject are for the most part at an everlasting stand.'[1]

Tense relations were again seen in 1621 when Parliament sought to give James advice on foreign policy and the proposed marriage of Charles to the Infanta of Spain. James immediately warned Parliament not to 'meddle with anything concerning our government or deep matters of state'. MPs in the House of Commons, stung by the rebuke, retorted in another petition that the King 'doth seem to abridge us of the ancient liberty of Parliament for freedom of speech … a liberty which we assure ourselves so wise and so just a king will not infringe, the same being our ancient and undoubted right, and an inheritance received from our ancestors.' Insensitively, James asserted that he was 'an old and experienced king needing no such lessons' and proceeded to instruct MPs that their privileges were in fact derived as a gift from the monarch. Infuriated, the MPs immediately drafted a Protestation in which they claimed their privileges as a birthright (see Voices from the past: The Commons' Protestation), only to have the king adjourn Parliament and tear the Protestation out of the Commons Journal with his own hands. A week later he dissolved Parliament.

Despite such high drama, what emerged between Crown and Parliament was something of a balancing act. The King's power was limited by the need to consult Parliament over key decisions in order for these to be passed into law. This balance of interests is what made the system work. Indeed, the ultimate expression of power in England was known as the 'King in Parliament', for only together could the two institutions fully exercise the full powers of government. Figure 1.3 is a contemporary representation of the 'King in Parliament'. It portrays James VI and I on his throne in the House of Lords with peers and bishops seated and MPs gathering at the entrance.

The practical balance of powers between Crown and Parliament was an important part of people's belief in England's **ancient constitution**. The concept of an ancient constitution was based on the idea that English people had a set of legal rights that had amassed over centuries. One important foundation block of the ancient constitution was Magna Carta, or 'The Great Charter', signed by King John in 1215 and reissued by various monarchs who followed. This document had sought to prevent the abuse of royal power and gave protection against illegal imprisonment without trial. Many English people saw Magna Carta as a resurrection of the ancient rights of English people dating back to Anglo-Saxon times. The idea that there existed basic laws and rights that prevented **tyrannical** rule by a monarch was an important one. This was reinforced by England's system of **Common Law**. The fact that monarchs swore to uphold the laws and customs of the realm as part of their coronation oath was thus significant. As we will see in the section on Ideas of royal authority, maintaining the ancient constitution was sometimes hard when asserting the divine right of the monarch to rule.

A key area of tension between James and his Parliaments was the reputation of his royal court. Well known for his extravagance, he used royal funds to grant gifts to his courtiers. Financial mismanagement was made worse by regular court scandals that centred round sexual deviance, corruption and even murder. This led critics in Parliament to term the king's favourites at court as 'spaniels to the king and wolves to the people'.[3] His willingness to place great power and wealth in their hands did much to provoke grumbles in Parliament. The best example of favouritism was George Villiers, a handsome young courtier upon whom James lavished land and title. From 1618, Villiers (later the Duke of Buckingham) handled much of the ageing King's business, including royal patronage (the granting of official posts and appointments). The homosexual nature of their relationship only served to further the idea that the royal court was morally corrupt. In 1614, the Addled Parliament spoke out against the corruption of the royal court and the King's abuse of his right to levy impositions (tax on trade). When it refused to grant new taxes to the King unless he ceased to raise impositions, it was dissolved. James's frustration is well represented in his private conversation with the Spanish ambassador (see Voices from the past: James VI and I to Gondomar, the Spanish Ambassador).

Although the relationship between James and his Parliaments caused tension, taken as a whole, his reign signified a period of relative political stability. David Smith has characterised their relationship as 'a rocky, at times verbally violent, yet essentially resilient marriage; despite the ups and downs a divorce was not on the cards'.[5]

## Relations with foreign powers

For much of his reign, James VI and I had pursued a peaceful foreign policy. James maintained peaceful relations with Spain by discussing the possibility of a marriage between his son, Prince Henry, and the Spanish Infanta. The so-called Spanish Match was even kept alive after Prince Henry's untimely death in 1612 by his brother, Prince Charles. Although the marriage was never settled, and was highly unpopular within Protestant England, James did well to use it as a means of maintaining peaceable diplomacy with Europe's greatest power. This relationship with Catholic Spain was balanced by his daughter Elizabeth's marriage to the Protestant Prince Frederick, Elector of the Palatinate (a German territory). In 1618, however, the peace of Europe was shattered when European Catholics and Protestants became embroiled in the **Thirty Years' War** (1618–48). James could only resist involvement for so long. Facing Parliamentary pressure, in 1624 he finally relented and sent an army to assist his daughter Elizabeth and his son-in-law, Frederick, reclaim their realm. The same year, Buckingham and Prince Charles had attempted a disastrous surprise visit to the Spanish Infanta in Madrid. The fiasco that this caused turned both men against the Spanish Match and ensured they supported Parliament's calls for war. By his death in 1625, James's kingdoms were once again at war with Spain.

**Figure 1.3:** James VI and I in Parliament. This print by Reginald Elstrack was published in 1608.

**ACTIVITY 1.1**

Read James VI and I's comments to the Spanish Ambassador in Voices from the past then consider the following questions.

1. What do James VI and I's remarks to the Spanish Ambassador reveal about his attitude towards Parliament?

2. Why might a historian doubt the sincerity of James VI and I's claims?

---

### Voices from the past

**James VI and I to Gondomar, the Spanish Ambassador, after his dismissal of the Addled Parliament of 1614**

The House of Commons is a body without a head. The members give their opinions in a disorderly manner. At their meeting nothing is heard but cries, shouts and confusion. I am surprised that my ancestors should ever have permitted such an institution to come into existence. But I am a stranger, and found it here when I arrived, so that I am obliged to put up with what I cannot get rid of.[4]

# Monarchy and Divine Right

Charles's older brother, Prince Henry, died from natural causes in 1612. He had been the epitome of a king-in-waiting, tall, athletic and handsome. His death had a profound impact on the 12-year-old Prince Charles and thrust him into the line of succession.

## The character and aims of Charles I

Charles was studious in nature but also persisted in riding and sports. Despite his small stature he could even take part in a joust without appearing ridiculous. He spoke with a Scottish accent and in conversation was thoughtful, taking his time to speak, partly in an attempt to overcome the stammer that afflicted his speech.

As he grew older his character revealed that he was a man of principle, unwilling to bend in his view if he believed he was right. Kevin Sharpe has contended that, 'while open to advice, his rigidity once he had made up his mind fostered the politics of inflexibility and principle rather than negotiation and compromise'.[6] Deeply loyal, he was wary of those who sought his affections, but once gained he would defend them to the last. He was often inaccessible to all but his closest advisors, and so confident was he in the virtue of his own beliefs that he often failed to explain himself clearly to his subjects or Parliament.

Many of Charles's aims as king were similar to those of his predecessors. Ireland, with a Catholic population often on the brink of rebellion, needed constant attention, and following the unification of the English and Scottish crowns under his father, Charles wanted to tighten their union. Key issues also remained in trying to balance the books by ensuring that money raised through parliamentary and non-parliamentary means would cover expenditure (see Figure 1.6). Unlike his father, Charles sought formality and order in his court and with it an end to the frivolous extravagance for which James's court had become notorious.

From a religious standpoint Charles was determined to safeguard the Protestant Church, not from its traditional enemy, the Catholics, but from what he saw as the damaging effects of fellow Protestants – the Puritans. Elizabeth I and James VI and I had allowed the Elizabethan Settlement to draw a veil over differences within the Church of England, tolerating a degree of freedom in the interpretation of the rules. Charles, however, clearly believed that Puritans, driven by their desire to rid the English Church of the last vestiges of Catholicism, threatened its unity. This led Charles to adopt a more conservative form of Protestantism, preserving some of the ceremony and hierarchy of the Catholic Church – the very things the Puritans despised. By defining his position so clearly Charles made enemies among the many other religious groups that existed. Nonetheless, with his characteristic determination Charles aimed to revive the beauty of religion by organising it along highly centralised, decorative, ceremonial lines.

Charles's political outlook was simple and he saw parliaments as a means to provide subsidies. He did not intend to justify his actions to them. Although Charles's uncompromising approach to relations with Parliament would ultimately cause major divisions, it is worth noting that his accession to the throne was the smoothest since that of Henry VIII in 1509, with many contemporaries commenting on the 'very gracious and affable' nature of the new king, and the Venetian ambassador commenting that 'the King observes a rule of great decorum'. The honeymoon period, however, was not destined to last for long.[7]

## The Queen and the court

Under Charles, the extravagant court life came to an end – economies were made, gift-giving was restricted and the Privy Council that advised the king was streamlined. The court became an expression of Charles's core values and in ceremonies and masques, Charles and his French queen, Henrietta Maria, appeared as the bringers of order, virtue and harmony.

Although the court played an important cultural role, bustling as it did with aspiring artists, musicians and scientists, it also provided an important political role. The court was a living community made up of Charles's and Henrietta Maria's advisors, ministers of state, clerks, secretaries, and leading gentlemen and nobles of the kingdom. It was at court that influence or position could be gained and, as the Duke of Buckingham found, if one moved in high enough circles, one might even gain the ear of the King himself. Courtiers tended to band together into informal factions, led by patrons (key figures or ministers with influence in government). The detached nature of court life from the day-to-day workings of Parliament and the fact that court life continued when Parliament was not sitting, troubled many MPs.

In time, one of the King's key advisors would be his queen, Henrietta Maria, whom he married in 1625. The marriage had served a diplomatic purpose and so it is therefore unsurprising that in the early years of their marriage they were distant figures. The Queen was desperately unhappy, not just with the dismissal of her French servants in 1626, but even more with her husband's preference for the advice of the Duke of Buckingham over hers. Yet despite this lack of practical influence over the King, many contemporaries believed the Queen exercised far more power than she did. This was symbolised in the suspension of the anti-Catholic recusancy fines following the King's marriage. Although this was part of the marriage terms, it came to symbolise the fear that many people had of the Catholic Queen's influence over her husband. Only after the assassination of Buckingham in 1628 did the couple develop bonds of genuine affection and love. The birth of a son, Prince Charles, in 1630 cemented their relationship and ensured that Henrietta Maria would become an important player in the events that would unfold in the decades to come (see the section on Charles I's Personal Rule in Chapter 2).

**Figure 1.4:** After the death of Buckingham, Charles and Henrietta Maria grew closer. She became a major influence at court.

## The King's advisors

One man who was to benefit from Charles's accession to the throne was Richard Montagu, a church rector from Essex. In the last years of James's reign Montagu had written and published controversial tracts on the nature of the Church of England. In his pamphlets, *A New Gag for an Old Goose* (1624) and *Appello Caesarem* (1625), Montagu argued against Puritanism in the Church; instead he maintained that the Church and its ceremonies were, and should be, closer to the Roman Catholic Church. These anti-Calvinist ideas were termed 'Arminian' after Jacobus Arminius (1560–1609), a Dutch theologian who advocated an increased role for Catholic-style ceremony, hierarchy and order in the Protestant Church. These ideas had caused major debate among MPs, especially Puritans like John Pym who argued that they caused 'disturbance in church and state'.[8] In July 1625, much to the annoyance of MPs, Charles appointed Montagu to the post of Royal Chaplain.

The greatest of Charles's advisors, however, was James's old favourite George Villiers, Duke of Buckingham. In 1623 Buckingham and Prince Charles had brought an end to the idea of the Spanish Match by visiting Madrid unannounced. On their return they had called for war against Spain and became the heroes of a Parliament eager for war. Although this support was only short-lived, Buckingham's influence over Charles remained until his murder in 1628. With characteristic loyalty, Charles never abandoned Buckingham, even when he was clearly becoming a figure of popular hatred.

## Ideas of royal authority

James VI and I had laid down his ideas about the nature of the **divine right of kings** in his book *Basilicon Doron*. Its preface urged his son to let its contents 'lie before you as a pattern'.[9] Charles seems to have taken it to heart, especially the instruction that he should be faithful to his conscience as it was inspired by God. Furthermore, it argued a king owed his position to God and thus was answerable only to God. That said, both James and Charles sought to rule in the public interest and for common good, both swearing to rule by the 'laws established' in their coronation oaths.[10]

There is little doubt that the vast majority of people at the time accepted the notion that God intended the monarch to reign. But the theory of divine right monarchy certainly gave some concern when taken to its ultimate extreme, as the monarch could theoretically do as he or she wished. This was certainly the impression that divine right, or 'absolutist', monarchs in France and Spain seemed to suggest. Thus the English were eager for the rights and liberties of English people to be maintained according to the law of the land. Most importantly, this meant consulting parliaments over key changes to the kingdom and in particular gaining parliamentary consent to raise taxes. Only Parliament could give permission for new taxes and this was known as 'granting supply' (see Figure 1.6).

> ### 🔑 Key term
>
> **divine right of kings:** the idea that authority was invested in monarchs by God, conferred on them by the religious ritual that was a royal coronation, and that they consequently answered only to God for the manner in which they exercised it.

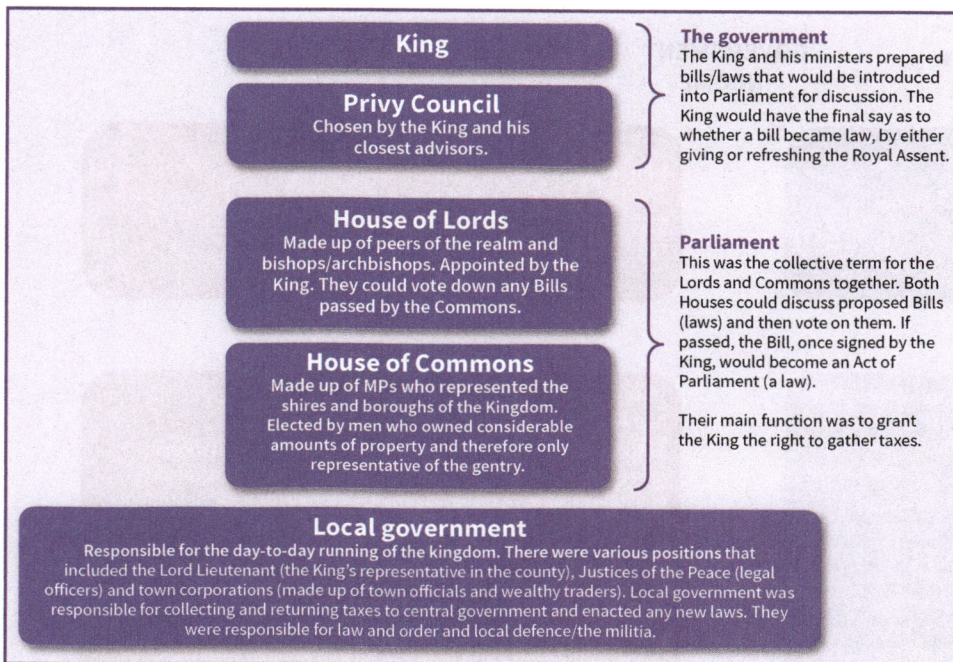

**Figure 1.5:** The Stuart system of government.

## Challenges to the arbitrary government of Charles I

Charles called three Parliaments between 1625 and the dissolution of his third Parliament in 1629. Despite Charles and Buckingham gaining the favour of MPs over their support for a war with Spain in the last year of James's life, this goodwill was soon lost.

### Reactions against financial policies

Clashes between Crown and Parliament soon occurred over finance. The cost of intervention in the Thirty Years War and conflict with Spain was made worse by the hurried alliance made with France in 1624. The alliance allowed for Charles to marry the French Princess Henrietta Maria but included a promise to help France defeat its Protestant rebels, the Huguenots of La Rochelle. The cheap and glorious naval raids reminiscent of Elizabeth's reign and dreamed of by Parliament had slipped away; Britain now had a costly land war and full-scale naval campaign on its hands.

As Charles's first Parliament assembled in June 1625 the King immediately called on MPs to provide funding to pay for the war that they had requested. Charles, however, was reluctant to explain the detail of war policy and so Parliament only passed a disappointing £140 000. In an unprecedented move it only granted Charles the right to collect tonnage and poundage for a year. Traditionally, Parliament granted a new monarch the right to collect tonnage and poundage for life; however, in this case it hoped this limit would encourage Charles to recall Parliament and bring about a full reform of customs duties, taxes and impositions. Instead, Charles saw this as an affront to his dignity. After adjourning the first Parliament to Oxford in order to avoid an outbreak of plague, its second session lasted a mere 10 days. Parliament refused to grant further supplies until the strategy for the war had been explained, and Charles, seeing war as a royal prerogative, was unwilling to explain himself to his subjects. With MPs demanding an enforcement of recusancy laws against Catholics and an enquiry into the sale of offices and titles by the King's favourite, Buckingham, Charles lost

**GOVERNMENT INCOME**

### Extraordinary Revenue
**Parliamentary means of raising finance**
This form of revenue was where the government received the majority of its income and made Parliament a key institution. When Parliament voted to give financial support to the monarch it was known as 'granting supply'.

### Ordinary Revenue
**Non-Parliamentary means of raising finance**
This form of revenue did not need to be granted by Parliament. It provided a much smaller income than parliamentary subsidies, but gave the monarch a degree of financial independence.

---

**Tonnage and poundage** – a customs tax on tradable goods. The right to raise this tax was traditionally granted to the monarch by Parliament for life. It ensured a regular income for the Crown for day-to-day running of the kingdom.

**Parliamentary subsidies** – a subsidy was a tax. MPs would decide on the amount that the monarch could raise (on average £100 000–£160 000). This would be divided between the counties and local assessors would calculate how much each of the monarch's subjects should pay. This normally depended on the amount of property owned. Collection of these taxes was a notoriously slow process and involved a high level of corruption, as unpaid officials took their expenses from the money collected. Sometimes people would attempt to avoid paying the tax altogether. This meant that in reality the full subsidy granted by Parliament was rarely received by the Exchequer in London.

---

**Purveyance** – this gave the monarch the right to buy goods at a highly discounted rate.

**Ship Money** – the right to raise this tax in times of national emergency was a prerogative of the monarch. It was raised in coastal counties in order to provide money for national defence.

**Wardship** – the right of the monarch to act as guardian to orphaned children of nobles and gentry. The Court of Wards would manage their estates until they came of age, and would benefit from the profits.

**Feudal dues** – ancient medieval taxes paid by tenants on royal lands, or by gentry and nobles who had been granted property by the monarch.

**Forest fines** – a tax on those who lived in, or near, royal forests.

**Forced Loan** – a tax that could be raised like a parliamentary subsidy in times of national emergency.

**Monopolies** – the monarch could sell the right to import and sell a certain product to a person or corporation. It allowed the person holding the monopoly to push prices up as there was no competition.

**Crown lands** – agricultural land owned by the Crown would produce an annual profit through rent or sale of crops. This land could also be sold.

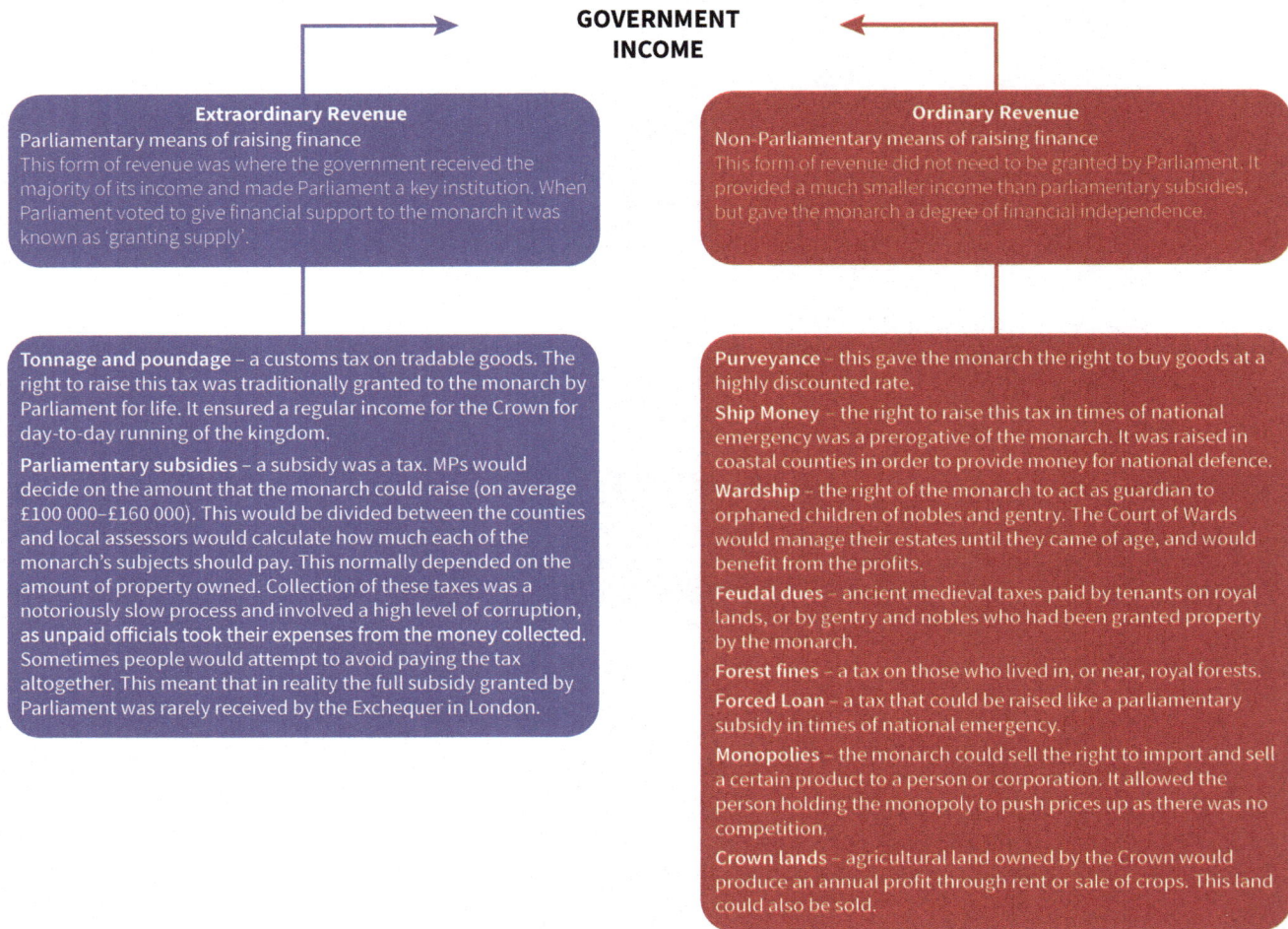

**Figure 1.6:** Sources of revenue available to the Crown.

patience and on 12 August he dissolved his first Parliament. Of major significance was the fact that the Tonnage and Poundage Bill had not been passed by the House of Lords by the time Parliament was dissolved, so when Charles began to raise this tax, he was doing so illegally.

When Parliament reassembled in February the next year, finance remained an obstacle to cooperation. The King hoped to avoid conflict through the shrewd tactic of appointing leading politicians, like Pym, to the post of sheriff in their respective counties, thus making them ineligible to sit as MPs. Despite this ingenious strategy, royal interference in elections was always controversial and so MPs remained critical. This time MPs were prepared to grant a generous £300 000 in subsidies but only on the condition that their grievances over religious and foreign policy be addressed (see the sections on Conflict over the Church and Reactions against foreign policy and the role of Buckingham). Charles's unwillingness to grant concessions was reinforced by the actions of MPs like Sir John Eliot and Sir Dudley Digges, both of whom led vicious verbal assaults on Buckingham's abuse of power and military failures in the war against Spain. At this point, Charles trespassed on parliamentary privilege by imprisoning Eliot, Digges and the Earl of Arundel for insolence in Parliament; however, following stern protests by Parliament, they were eventually released. With

MPs beginning to arrange for an impeachment of Buckingham, Charles, no money having been granted, dissolved his second Parliament to prevent the impeachment from proceeding.

Between 1626 and 1628, with his coffers empty, Charles continued to raise tonnage and poundage without parliamentary consent, imprisoning anyone who refused to pay. His need for finance also saw him resort to raising a Forced Loan (see Figure 1.6). Although the monarch had the right to raise taxes without parliamentary consent in moments of national emergency, such a move was perceived by many as being an abuse of royal power. Importantly, however, there were key figures newly appointed in the Church who preached and encouraged payment of the Forced Loan. This was significant as it connected Arminianism with the more arbitrary approach to government.

Further worries over royal disregard for the 'laws established' were revealed in the Five Knights' Case of 1627 when Charles imprisoned five knights for refusing to pay the Forced Loan. The knights claimed they had been arrested without just cause and that the emergency powers of the monarch did not, and should not, extend to arresting subjects without cause. The judges ruled in favour of the King but stopped short of stating that the monarch had an *absolute* right to imprison – this was important, because it ensured that the monarch still needed to act within the law. Despite this, the case was enough to make many feel that Common Law was no longer being respected.

In the meantime, Buckingham's inept handling of foreign policy had seen England slip into a disastrous war with France (see the section on Reactions against foreign policy and the role of Buckingham) and ensured that another Parliament was needed to provide further supplies. Thus, the stage was set for Charles's third and final Parliament.

## Conflict over the Church

In Charles's early parliaments, clashes over finance were coupled with those over the Church of England. During the first Parliament in 1625 concerns were heightened by Charles's marriage to Henrietta Maria and the promotion of Richard Montagu to the post of Royal Chaplain (see the section on The King's advisors). Charles, it seemed, was increasingly willing to move the Church away from the broad Church maintained by his predecessors, and instead shift it towards the ceremony and order favoured by Arminians like Montagu (this could be misinterpreted as a step towards Catholicism). For Charles, the Protestant Church of England needed to reflect order and hierarchy and thus needed uniformity to be imposed across the realm. This shift was unpopular not only with Puritans, but also with moderate Anglicans who feared that such a move could lead to schism (division) in the Church of England.

Charles's determination to promote Arminianism seemed to be confirmed in February 1626 when Buckingham chaired a theological debate at York House in London. The debate had been called at the request of the Earl of Warwick in the hope of

**Key term**

**grievances:** the period term used to describe complaints. Grievances were raised by MPs in 1640–42 following the Personal Rule, and by the army following the First Civil War.

**ACTIVITY 1.2**

Read Sibthorpe in Voices from the past and then consider the questions below.

1. According to Sibthorpe, why should people pay the Forced Loan?

2. How was Sibthorpe's reasoning linked to the concept of divine right monarchy?

3. Having read the section on Ideas of royal authority, why would many have opposed Sibthorpe's argument?

**Voices from the past**

### *Robert Sibthorpe*

Sibthorpe, an Arminian member of the clergy, supported the king's attempt to raise a Forced Loan in 1626. In a sermon that was later published, he preached:

'If a prince imposed an immoderate, yea and unjust tax, yet the subject may not thereupon withdraw his obedience and duty. Nay, he is bound in conscience to submit, as under the scourge of sin.'

persuading Charles and Buckingham to abandon the anti-Calvinist Arminians in favour of a maintaining the broader Church that would accommodate Puritans. The King, however, was unmoved, and Buckingham strongly defended the writings of the Arminian Royal Chaplain, Richard Montagu. This was a huge disappointment to men like Warwick and Viscount Saye and Sele, who held Puritan and Calvinist sympathies. Far from calming their fears by convicting Montagu for Arminian heresy, the York House debate had confirmed the King's support for the Arminian cause and thus began to split opinion in a way that the old broad Church of the Elizabethan Settlement had not. The debates also heightened tensions in Parliament, spurring on the attacks on Buckingham. By 1628, just as the third Parliament assembled, Montagu was created Bishop of Chichester and his fellow Arminian, William Laud, was appointed Bishop of London; it seemed the lines were becoming even more clearly drawn.

So it was that in the second, and final, session of Charles's third Parliament, in 1629, MPs drafted a set of **Resolutions** on Religion. The Resolutions argued vehemently against the Arminian faction and urged the King to give more moderate men appointments in the Church. Alas, their pleas fell on deaf ears and as we will see in the section on The dissolution of Parliament and the King's commitment to Personal Rule, Parliament was dissolved before any further steps could be taken to challenge the rise of Laud and Arminianism.

## Reactions against foreign policy and the role of Buckingham

Quarrels over finance and religion defined the mood of Charles's first three parliaments. However, it was foreign policy that encouraged violent attacks on the King's chief advisor, Buckingham. Despite having given Parliament the war it had wanted, Buckingham failed as a military commander and in late 1625 he oversaw a shambolic and wasteful naval raid on Cadiz. As soon as Charles called his second Parliament in 1626 in order to pay for losses incurred by the military campaign, MPs levelled their anger at Buckingham's mismanagement of the fleet in his capacity as Lord High Admiral. It was these charges of criminal abuse of power, corruption and negligence of the country's defences aimed at Buckingham that led Charles to infringe upon parliamentary privilege by imprisoning the MPs Eliot and Digges, both of whom led the attacks. Although they were later released, the loyalty Buckingham enjoyed from his sovereign was clearly leading to tension between Crown and Parliament. Neither side was willing to give way, and Charles's eventual decision to dissolve his second Parliament in June 1626 resulted from the fact that he refused to dismiss Buckingham simply to appease Parliament's anger and distrust.

In light of this hostility towards Buckingham, it was perhaps misguided of Charles to allow the Duke to fill the Privy Council with his own supporters in the months that followed. Indeed, the situation was further compounded in 1627 when Buckingham's inept handling of diplomacy let Britain slip into a war it could ill afford with France: Charles was now at war with both the major continental Catholic powers. The significance of this was threefold. First, it made the need for parliamentary subsidies more acute. Second, Buckingham's continued failings in military affairs, this time the fiasco at the siege of La Rochelle, increased MPs' demands for his dismissal or impeachment. Finally, it ensured that Charles's stubborn loyalty became a political problem. His fervent defence of his favourite meant that MPs' attacks on Buckingham came close to personal criticism of Charles himself. All of this became abundantly clear during the third Parliament in 1628 when once again the MPs Eliot and Coke led the charge against Buckingham, whom they termed 'the grievance of grievances' and 'the cause of all our miseries'.[11] To Charles, this was an affront to his royal will and personal dignity.

In the end, fate played a hand. On 23 August, just as he was preparing for a renewed expedition to La Rochelle, Buckingham was stabbed to death by a demobbed soldier, John Felton. His sudden and unexpected death should have given Charles a chance to open a new chapter in his relations with Parliament. However, the chance was missed and Charles, ignoring the widespread public rejoicing at the Duke's death, continued with Buckingham's policies. Buckingham's murder was the act of an individual pursuing a personal vendetta, yet Charles saw it as symptomatic of the political imbalance in the nation, and this strengthened his resolve to stand fast in defence of his royal prerogatives.

# Parliamentary radicalism

For many MPs the Duke of Buckingham had become the symbol of wider grievances, most notably financial mismanagement, disregard for Common Law and a dangerous shift in favour of Arminianism in the Church.

## Personalities and policies of parliamentary opposition to the King

Two of the key leaders of parliamentary opposition during the 1620s were Sir John Eliot and Sir Dudley Digges. One of their main priorities was to remove Buckingham, who in their eyes corrupted the relationship between Charles and his subjects. In the articles of impeachment drawn up against Buckingham in 1626, Eliot argued that 'Our honour is ruined, our ships are sunk, our men are perished; not by the sword, not by the enemy, not by chance but by those we trust'.[12]

If Eliot's criticism was fuelled by the chaos he had seen in the aftermath of Buckingham's military campaigns (Eliot was Vice-Admiral for Devon), others like the MP Sir Edward Coke were driven more by constitutional worries. In 1628 Coke, himself a lawyer, was responsible for drafting the *Petition of Right* (which is fully explored in the next section). This documents that critics were most concerned with restoring the old constitutional balance between Crown and Parliament.

Indeed, it was the desire to defend the constitutional balance of powers that lay at the heart of opposition to the King's government. Coke had long challenged the idea that divine right gave the monarch complete freedom of action. Rather, Coke maintained that English Common Law was the highest authority in the land, to which even the monarch was subject. This did not mean Coke was anti-monarchy or a republican; he argued that the English monarchy existed within clear boundaries, and it was imperative for monarchs to uphold their coronation oath to rule by, and uphold, the laws of the realm.

In the eyes of critics like Eliot, Digges and Coke, the tendency of James and Charles to assert their royal prerogatives threatened the balance of the ancient constitution. As we have seen, the attack by Eliot and Digges on the King's favourite, Buckingham, had led to their illegal imprisonment in 1626, and Coke too had been imprisoned for eight months in the Tower of London for his part in drafting the Protestation of 1621 that asserted the rule of law and parliamentary privileges as 'the ancient … birthright and inheritance of the subjects of England'. The fact that they were dealt with in such a way, and contrary to their parliamentary privilege of immunity to arrest, only reinforced their worries.

Thus, the political opposition faced by Charles in his early parliaments arose chiefly from fears that the ancient constitution and the rule of law were slowly being undermined and concern was fuelled by growing concern about the King's advance of Arminianism. In the 1620s Buckingham came to be the symbol of the people's deepest constitutional and religious fears.

## The Petition of Right

Against the backdrop of Buckingham's disastrous military campaign against the French, Charles called his third Parliament in March 1628. MPs realised that if they refused to grant supplies to the King again there was a real risk of permanent dissolution. To avoid this, the MPs resisted an attack on the King's advisors and instead created the **Petition of Right**, which outlined the constitutional rules by which the nation should be governed. In carefully stating the law, the Petition made clear the principle that taxation could not be raised without parliamentary consent. It also stated that the law was sacred and needed to be upheld by the monarch. The MPs were clearly hoping that the Petition of Right would provide a clear basis for agreement between the King and his Parliament. The petition was clever, as MPs were suggesting that these things were principles that already existed and merely needed clarification. Once accepted, the Petition of Right would carry the weight of statutory law, and thus could not be ignored. On 2 June 1628 Charles issued a response to the Petition that evaded outright acceptance, but five days later he evidently changed his mind and accepted the Petition in full. The gleeful MPs, confident that the Petition of Right carried the weight of statute law, dutifully passed a Bill allowing Charles to collect five subsidies.

However, within a year it became clear that Charles did not see the Petition as legally binding. When it was printed, he not only instructed the royal printer to include a version of his initial response (avoiding outright acceptance of the Petition) but he also had its statute number removed, thus creating uncertainty over its status as a law. The King did not believe that the Petition prevented him from collecting tonnage and poundage without parliamentary consent, and when MPs issued a remonstrance claiming that doing so was 'a breach of the fundamental liberties of this kingdom', the king promptly prorogued (suspended) Parliament. In a short speech to MPs, Charles confirmed his acceptance of the Petition of Right but asserted that he owed 'the account of [his] actions to God alone'.[14] The Petition of Right had failed to draw both sides together. In the following months, as Charles continued to collect tonnage and poundage, one MP and merchant, John Rolle, refused to pay and the King ordered his goods confiscated. The importance of this act would become clear once MPs reassembled in 1629.

## The dissolution of Parliament and the King's commitment to Personal Rule

The second session of the third Parliament began on 20 January 1629 and once again the King asked MPs to confirm his right to collect tonnage and poundage. Once more the MPs stalled, demanding that their grievances over the Petition of Right, the rise of Arminianism and the Rolle case be addressed first. Parliament felt that the confiscation of Rolle's goods as punishment for refusing to pay tonnage and poundage was a breach of parliamentary privilege, just as it would have been if he had been arrested himself. Rumours began to circulate that Charles was preparing to dissolve Parliament unless he got his way. Thus, on 2 March, two of Eliot's allies in the Commons decided that desperate times called for desperate measures. In a dramatic act, they physically pinned the Speaker of the House of Commons in his chair and locked the door of the chamber until MPs had passed a **protestation**. This protestation became known as The Three Resolutions and declared that any person attempting to reform the Church along Popish or Arminian lines would be a 'capital enemy' to the state, and that anyone who levied or paid tonnage and poundage without parliamentary consent was a 'capital enemy [...] of the liberties of England'.[15] Each resolution was met with shouts of approval. Outraged, Charles immediately dissolved the Parliament, vowing not to call another until those that had been misled by Eliot and the other 'vipers' understood the error of their ways.[16]

### Key term

The **Petition of Right**, 1628:[13]

Presented to the king by Parliament. The document outlined the following principles:

- The king or Privy Council cannot imprison a subject without just cause in the eyes of the law.
- No tax (in whatever form) can be collected without Parliament's consent.
- No soldiers can be billeted in people's homes against their will.

### Key term

**protestation:** the process by which MPs expressed their dislike of a policy, person or action. It would be passed by a vote.

Thus ended the last of Charles's early parliaments. Charles believed he was within his rights, but he was content that it had quelled Puritan troublemaking, and provided 'a solution to the problem posed by the plotting of "envenomed spirits which troubled … the blessed harmony between us and our subjects"'.[17]

## Further reading

An excellent outline of the period and the background to Charles's reign can be found in Coward B. *The Stuart Age: England 1603–1714*. London: Longman; 1994. A shorter introduction can be found in Morrill J. *Stuart Britain: A Very Short Introduction*. Oxford: Oxford University Press; 2000. For a classic biography of Charles I see Hibbert C. *Charles I: A Life of Religion, War and Treason*. London: Palgrave Macmillan; 2007. An excellent outline of events can be found in Smith DL. *The Stuart Parliaments, 1603–1689*. London: Arnold; 1999.

### Practice essay questions

1. 'Disputes over finance were the main reason for conflict between Crown and Parliament in the years 1625–29.' Explain why you agree or disagree with this view.
2. 'The growing strength of the Puritan faction in Parliament was mainly responsible for opposition to Charles reign, 1625–29.' Explain why you agree or disagree with this view.
3. 'Conflict between Crown and Parliament was always likely, 1625–29.' Assess the validity of this view.
4. With reference to these extracts and your understanding of the historical context, of these is two sources is more valuable in explaining the relationship between Crown and Parliament on the accession of Charles I?

## Extract A

James VI and I to Gondomar, the Spanish Ambassador, after the King's dismissal of the Addled Parliament of 1614.

The House of Commons is a body without a head. The members give their opinions in a disorderly manner. At their meeting nothing is heard but cries, shouts and confusion. I am surprised that my ancestors should ever have permitted such and institution to come into existence. But I am a stranger, and found it here when I arrived, so that I am obliged to put up with what I cannot get rid of.[18]

## Extract B

The Commons' Protestation, 18 December 1621.

The liberties of Parliament are the ancient and undoubted birthright and inheritance of the subject of England; and affairs concerning the King, State, and defence of the realm and the of the Church of England, and the maintenance and making of laws and redress of grievances are proper subjects and matters of counsel and debate in Parliament.[19]

> ## 📎 Chapter summary
>
> By the end of this chapter you should have gained a broad overview of how and why tensions were beginning to rise between the King and his Parliament. You should also understand:
>
> - the ideology upon which divine right monarchy was based
> - the reasons for opposition to arbitrary government and the extent to which they were widespread or successful
> - the role played by Charles's advisors
> - the significance of Laud's religious reforms
> - the reasons for Charles's decision to dissolve Parliament and embark on Personal Rule.

## End notes

1  The text of the Form of Apology and Satisfaction can be found in Tanner JR. *Constitutional Documents of the Reign of James I*. Cambridge: CUP; 1930. p. 217–30 (as corrected by Elton GR).

2  Tanner JR. *English Constitutional Conflicts of the Seventeenth Century 1603–1689*. Cambridge: CUP; 1971. p. 49.

3  Houston SJ. *James I*. London: Routledge; 1995. p. 45.

4  Smith DL. *The Stuart Parliaments, 1603–1689*. London: Arnold; 1999. p. 103.

5  Smith DL. *The Stuart Parliaments, 1603–1689*. p. 103.

6  Sharpe K. *Stuart Monarchy and Political Culture*. In Morrill J. (ed.) *The Oxford Illustrated History of Tudor and Stuart Britain*. Oxford: OUP; 1996. p. 249.

7  Quoted in Smith DL. *A History of the Modern British Isles, 1603–1707*. p. 67–68

8  Ibid. p. 68. Also see p. 63 for Montagu's tracts.

9  *Basilicon Doron*, quoted in Cust R. *Charles I: A Political Life*. London: Pearson; 2007. p. 29 and Ashley M. *The English Civil War*. Stroud: Sutton History Paperbacks; 1997. p. 12.

10 Cust R. *Charles I: A Political Life*. London: Pearson; 2007. p. 29 and Ashley M. *The English Civil War*. Stroud: Sutton History Paperbacks; 1997. p. 20.

11 Quoted in Smith DL. *A History of the Modern British Isles, 1603–1707*. p. 73.

12 Quoted in Gregg P. *King Charles I*. Oakland: University of California Press; 1984. p. 144–45.

13 Key points drawn from the Petition of Right quoted in Gardiner SR (ed.) *The Constitutional Documents of the Puritan Revolution 1625–1660*. Oxford: OUP; 1889. p. 1–5.

14 Quoted in Smith DL. *A History of the Modern British Isles, 1603–1707*. p. 73.

15 Quoted in Hibbert C. *Charles I: A Life of Religion, War and Treason*. London: Palgrave Macmillan; 2007; p. 107. Also, Smith DL. *A History of the Modern British Isles, 1603–1707*. p. 73.

16 Gregg P. *King Charles I*. p. 186.

17 Braddick M. *God's Fury, England's Fire: A New History of the English Civil Wars*. London: Penguin Books; 2009. p. 56.

18 Smith DL. *The Stuart Parliaments*, 1603–1689. p. 103.

19 Tanner JR. *English Constitutional Conflicts of the Seventeenth Century 1603–1689*.

# 2 An experiment in Absolutism, 1629–1640

In this section we will examine the 11 years in which Charles ruled without a Parliament. We will look into:

- Charles I's Personal Rule: Charles I's chief ministers; methods of government; financial policies and the reaction against them.
- Religious issues: Laud and Arminianism in England and Scotland; the growth of opposition from Puritans.
- Political issues: the role of Wentworth; policies in Ireland and England; the reactions against the Crown; demands for the recall of Parliament.
- Radicalism, dissent and the approach of war: the spread of religious radicalism; the Scottish National Covenant and the First Bishops' War; the Pacification of Berwick; the Second Bishops' war.

## Introduction

This chapter explores the 11 years in which Charles I ruled without a parliament. When Charles had dismissed Parliament in 1629 there was no clear plan for how he would rule. However, key individuals soon rose to power as chief advisors to the King. With his lands at peace, Charles settled down to bring reform to the Church and ever closer unity between England and Scotland. To fund his endeavours he was forced to raise taxes without parliamentary consent and fears arose that he was fast becoming an absolutist monarch. Perhaps more divisive was the belief that his reforms put England's Protestantism at risk.

This was a period of controversy and intrigue at the time and has been ever since. Critics of Charles, most notably Whig historians such as Macaulay and Trevelyan, traditionally termed this period the Eleven Years' Tyranny. However, more recent analysis has highlighted the logic of efforts made by Charles and his advisors to establish a reformed and centralised state. Consequently, the period is now less divisively referred to as the Personal Rule.

## Timeline

| | |
|---|---|
| 1629 | **14 April:** Treaty of Susa ends war with France |
| 1630 | **28 January:** Distraint of Knighthood introduced<br>**August:** Exchequer judges confirm the King's right to impose knighthood fines<br>**5 November:** Treaty of Madrid ends war with Spain |
| 1632 | **12 January:** Thomas Wentworth appointed Lord Deputy of Ireland |
| 1633 | **February:** William Prynne sent to the Tower for publishing *Histriomastix*<br>**June–July:** Charles visits Scotland; crowned at Holyrood<br>**23 July:** Wentworth arrives in Dublin<br>**6 August:** Laud nominated as Archbishop of Canterbury<br>**November:** St Gregory's Case; King and Privy Council rule that the bishop should have the right to decide the position of communion tables within each diocese<br>Charles and Laud restrict use of sermons |
| 1634 | **May:** Prynne's first trial; sentenced to lose his ears<br>**Summer:** forest fines imposed<br>**October:** Ship Money levied on coastal towns and counties<br>**12 December:** Charles admits first papal agent to court since 1558 |
| 1635 | **August:** Ship Money extended to inland counties; levied annually until 1639 |
| 1637 | **June:** trial of Burton, Prynne and Bastwick<br>**23 July:** Scottish Prayer Book introduced<br>**November:** John Hampden's case |
| 1638 | **February:** trial of Lilburne for circulating Puritan literature; National Covenant drawn up in Scotland<br>**September:** Charles withdraws the Scottish Prayer Book and agrees to call Scottish Parliament General Assembly<br>**November:** Scottish General Assembly abolishes episcopacy |
| 1639 | **June:** First Bishops' War; Pacification of Berwick<br>**Summer–autumn:** growing resistance to payment of Ship Money; only £43 417 paid out of £214 000 assessed, compared with a yield of over 90% in the year October 1637–September 1638<br>**22 September:** Wentworth arrives in England |
| 1640 | **13 April–5 May:** Short Parliament; Convocation passes 17 canons<br>**20 August:** Second Bishops' War begins<br>**28 August:** Scots rout English forces at Newburn; 12 peers petition Charles to recall Parliament<br>**24 September:** Great Council of Peers at York<br>**21 October:** Truce of Ripon; Scots receive £850 a day and remain in the northeast of England until a settlement is agreed and confirmed by the English Parliament |

# Charles I's Personal Rule

With Parliament dissolved in March 1629, Charles fell back on the support of his key advisors, as well as his wife and consort, Queen Henrietta Maria. The Queen's influence is hard to quantify but it grew after the death of Buckingham in 1628. Although there is no evidence to suggest Charles was swayed by Henrietta Maria's Catholic faith, he certainly did indulge it. By 1636 a new Catholic chapel had been constructed at Somerset House in London and at Court the Queen cultivated a Catholic faction. Above all, her well-known enjoyment of masques, lavish entertainments and theatre became a symbol of something rotten at the heart of government and gave fuel to popular fears of a Catholic conspiracy. The Queen's love of French theatre in which women appeared in women's roles, and the parts she played in masques, elicited the **'seditious libels'** aimed at her by the Puritan William Prynne, for which he was mutilated and branded in 1634. Well accustomed to French **absolutism**, the Queen urged firmness and despite her growing unpopularity, Henrietta Maria's position ensured she exerted influence over her husband.

The Queen's Catholic faction at Court stirred particular concern. In a worrying public display of their faith these English Catholics attended the Queen's Chapel. In reality it is hard to discern the influence Catholics managed to exert; however, the problem was the 'fatal suspicion' with which people began to view the Court.[1]

## Charles I's chief ministers

### Archbishop Laud

Although no great supporter of the Queen, one of Charles's most trusted advisors was William Laud. Laud had risen from obscurity, the son of a clothier from Reading. Having attended grammar school and Oxford University he had worked his way up through the Church hierarchy. With the help of Buckingham's **patronage**, by 1626 he had been appointed Bishop of Bath and Wells and Dean of the Chapel Royal, and two years later he was appointed Bishop of London. It was from this position that Laud began to build a following within the Church. These Laudian reformers were keen to defend the Church of England from Puritanism and in 1633 Laud was appointed Archbishop of Canterbury. Laud was an Arminian. His reforms to decoration and ceremony sought to return a sense of sanctity and beauty to the Church of England. He distrusted the innovation of Puritan worship and preaching. Laud became the most important enforcer of Charles's attempt to achieve religious uniformity across his kingdoms.

### Sir Thomas Wentworth (later Earl of Stafford)

Charles found another stalwart supporter in the guise of the formidable Thomas Wentworth. In many ways Wentworth was an unlikely champion of the King's Personal Rule. As an MP he had been a vocal critic of Buckingham and in 1628 he had been a keen supporter of the Petition of Right. However, having achieved acceptance of the Petition and fearful that the balance of England's ancient constitution was being undermined, Wentworth became increasingly supportive of the Crown. In recognition of his stance, Wentworth was raised to the peerage, created a Privy Councillor and appointed to run the Council of the North in York. In 1632 he received his most important position as Lord Deputy of Ireland, from where he was later recalled to help Charles deal with the crises unfolding in Scotland and England.

## Methods of government

To rule without a parliament was not unheard of. Parliaments tended to be called at moments of financial necessity (Elizabeth called only 10 parliaments in her whole reign) and thus Charles was forced to rely heavily on local government in the **shires**

**ACTIVITY 2.1**

Why do you think MPs came to hate Wentworth so much? When you read about his policies later in the chapter, you should add more detail to your answer.

**Key term**

**seditious libel:** a criminal offence in which the written word is used to encourage insurrection against established authorities or to change the established Church and state by unlawful means.

**Key term**

**absolutism:** a form of monarchy where the King exercises total power without recourse to a parliament. Their power extends beyond the law.

**Key term**

**patronage:** the process whereby somebody receives the support of a social or political superior.

**Figure 2.1:** Thomas Wentworth, Lord Deputy of Ireland.

## Key term

**borough:** an administrative element found normally describing a self-governing town or part of a larger city. Boroughs would often have the right to return their own MPs to Parliament.

## Key term

**militia:** soldiers raised by the lords lieutenant of the counties in moments of local or national emergency. The militia were part-time soldiers, often poorly trained and lacking motivation.

### ACTIVITY 2.2

Using the information in the section on Charles I's Personal Rule, write a brief fact file on:

1. Henrietta Maria
2. William Laud
3. Thomas Wentworth

### ACTIVITY 2.3

Having read the section on Methods of government, create a spider diagram to show the methods used by Charles to govern without Parliament.

and **boroughs** of the kingdom to enforce his will. The nobility and gentry occupied positions as lords lieutenant, sheriffs, assize judges, justices of the peace (JPs) and local officials. In the absence of a parliament, this network, supplemented by the Church hierarchy and courts, continued the practical enforcement of government. The local elite collected taxes, oversaw the maintenance, training and deployment of the **militia**, implemented social and economic legislation, oversaw the trial of most criminals and, increasingly, enforced religious uniformity.

Charles's reliance on local institutions is perhaps best revealed in his circulation of the *Book of Orders* to sheriffs and magistrates in 1630 and 1631. Although specifically designed to give practical instruction on how to deal with economic hardship and poor relief, its very existence reveals the reliance on local government. This was also echoed in the *Declaration of Sports*, a directive issued by Charles to ensure that Puritan zeal did not illegally prohibit sporting recreation on Sundays.[2]

The courts system operated alongside local institutions. At a local level the most important element of this system was the JP. As well as presiding over the county courts and their policing roles, JPs were increasingly the recipients of administrative orders from the Privy Council. Legally, Charles's Personal Rule was further supported by a series of national courts termed prerogative courts, who sat in the name of the monarch. The Court of Exchequer Chamber, consisting of 12 judges, was appointed by the monarch and enforced the raising of revenue. The Court of Star Chamber, made up of Privy Councillors and judges sat in judgement on high-profile cases free from the norms expected in a Common Law trial. These prerogative courts had originated in the medieval period as a means of helping the monarch deal with over-mighty nobles who posed a threat to the Crown and so needed to be dealt with swiftly. By the 1630s their function had changed and they were increasingly used as a heavy-handed way of silencing critics of royal policy.

The dual process of using heavy-handed legal enforcement and demanding much of the local officials became known as the policy of 'thorough government'. It was a term used by both Wentworth and Laud and came to define their approach to government. 'Thorough' was an attempt to make government more efficient, prevent waste, maximise income and remove any local officials who were not up to the job. It also ensured that the central government interfered more in local affairs. During the Personal Rule, Wentworth and Laud introduced inspections of militia, reissued the *Book of Orders* and the *Declaration of Sports*, and initiated Bishops' 'visitations' to check that the parish clergy were enacting Laud's reforms. Anyone who did not conform could expect to either be removed from their post or held accountable before a prerogative court like Star Chamber or the Council of the North. (See the sections on Religious issues and Political issues later in this chapter for more detail on the policy of 'thorough'.)

## Financial policies and the reaction against them

Richard Weston was one of Charles's key ministers. During his early political career he served as an MP and diplomat. Despite his Catholic faith, Weston achieved the important position of Lord Treasurer. He successfully helped engineer peace with France (1629) and Spain (1630), limited government spending, reformed tax-raising procedures and maintained the financing of government through non-parliamentary sources. His single-minded approach, coupled with his creative use of old fundraising methods ensured that by Weston's death in 1635, Charles was able to rule without the need for parliamentary subsidies.

Weston relied on Charles's prerogative rights to raise what was termed 'ordinary revenue'. This was made up of a series of measures that included impositions or Forced Loans worth £200 000 per annum; an increase in the revenue gained from wards of Court (the estates of orphaned nobles held in trust by the Crown); stricter enforcement of recusancy fines against Catholics who failed to attend Church of England services; avoidance of the 1624 Monopolies Act by selling monopolies to companies rather than individuals (the so-called Popish Soap monopoly was worth £29 000 per year); Distraint of Knighthood, which raised up to £174 000 a year by fining gentlemen of property who had failed to fulfil an ancient custom of presenting themselves for knighthoods at the coronation; forest fines imposed on individuals who had encroached on the ancient boundaries of royal forests; the raising of **tonnage and poundage** (import duties) without parliamentary consent; and most importantly from 1634, Ship Money, a levy on the coastal counties for naval defence in moments of emergency, extended to inland counties in 1635 and raised annually from then on.[3]

Most taxes are met with a grumble, and it is certain that Charles's methods were no exception. Reviving the Distraint of Knighthood and forest fines frustrated the gentry. Similarly, the revival of monopolies did much to anger traders, as competition was stifled and costs rose. Some historians have argued that Charles was trying to instigate **tyrannical** absolutism, using financing methods that would negate the need for Parliament. Indeed, Charles's decision to levy Ship Money annually could indicate his intention to use this as a regular replacement for parliamentary subsidies. Indeed, his collection of tonnage and poundage without parliamentary consent only confirms this suspicion.

Alternatively, one might argue that Charles hoped to facilitate what Laud and Wentworth termed 'thorough' government. Indeed, Parliament's refusal to grant Charles the right to raise tonnage and poundage for life (as was the custom upon the accession of a new monarch) was a greater constitutional innovation than Charles's decision to raise it without their consent. Whatever your view, the King's methods were legally dubious and his intent unclear. Charles's reluctance to explain himself ensured that his actions were open to misinterpretation.

## Ship Money

Although there was no widespread outcry against the King's methods, it was Ship Money that proved most contentious. There were some high-profile opponents to Ship Money, such as Viscount Saye and Sele, a man who would become a prominent Parliamentarian in the 1640s. However, it was John Hampden who launched the strongest challenge to the collection of Ship Money in 1637.

A gentleman from Buckinghamshire, John Hampden had already been imprisoned in 1627 for refusing to pay the Forced Loan. In 1635 he had refused to pay the £1 assessment on his estates for the collection of Ship Money. In 1637, the case was taken to the Court of Exchequer Chamber where Hampden's case rested on the argument that Ship Money was illegal as the kingdom was not in a state of emergency. The 12 judges ruled in Charles's favour by seven to five. However, many saw the split in the judges as a moral victory for Hampden. It had an impact on popular opinion and some local officials charged with implementing the policy even refused to take up their posts.[4]

In contrast, there was some support for Ship Money. The revenue facilitated a hugely successful rebuilding of the navy and in Yorkshire, for example, the people of Scarborough willingly fulfilled their assessment, happy in the knowledge that the new warships would protect them from French privateers that lurked off the coast and frustrated local commerce. More generally, over 90% of Ship Money was collected. It was only when war clouds gathered in Scotland in 1639, and then in Ireland in 1641, that non-parliamentary revenue began to fail. Coupled with the raising of **coat and conduct money**, the collection of Ship Money became increasingly difficult and from 1639 revenue began to drop dramatically.

**Key term**

**tonnage and poundage:** a customs tax on tradable goods. The right to raise this tax was traditionally granted to the King by Parliament for life.

**ACTIVITY 2.4**

In a two-column table, list the reasons why people challenged or supported the financial policies used in the Personal Rule.

ACTIVITY 2.5

Why would Puritans have seen Arminian reforms as dangerous?

## Religious issues

The year 1633, in which Laud was made Archbishop of Canterbury, marked a moment of change. The notion of the world as a battleground between good and evil, between God and the Devil, was not lost on the people. Yet the Elizabethan Settlement led many to hope that division and schism were now behind them as it continued to offer sufficient freedom to allow a range of Protestant believers to be accommodated under its auspices in exchange for outward conformity to Anglican worship. Although the Gunpowder Plot of 1605 did much to increase the pressures placed on Catholics during James's reign, the realm Charles I had inherited was one in which a broad national Church encompassed a spectrum of religious convictions.

We must be careful, however, not to overestimate the tranquility brought about by the Elizabethan Settlement. Latent fears of Catholic attempts to subvert and overthrow the English Reformation continued to haunt people's imagination. The English Church had also been divided over the Calvinist doctrine of predestination – the idea that every individual is already destined for heaven or hell. Some believed that salvation could be gained through living a virtuous life; God's grace would be earned. Others, notably Puritans, believed that humans were so sinful that only the 'elect' few were predestined to ascend to heaven. These godly people were identifiable by their lifestyle, plainness of dress and lack of pride and greed. Eager to prove their credentials as God's elect, Puritans believed fiercely in the need to preach God's word to an erring flock of the damned. Puritans believed that any of God's elect, whether a member of the clergy or a **layperson**, could preach sermons inspired by the word of God as contained in the Bible; this should not be the preserve of appointed clergy regurgitating set prayers laid down by bishops. To others, however, especially the mainstream of the Anglican Church and the established episcopacy, Puritan approaches appeared dangerously **zealous** and innovative. Indeed, in the years leading up to the Civil Wars, the words 'zeal' and 'innovation' became loaded terms that threatened to undermine the hierarchy of the Church and the established social and political order that it supported.

### Laud and Arminianism in England and Scotland

It was against this backdrop that Laud introduced his Arminian reforms and in so doing opened up all the points of religious contention that had hitherto been allowed to go unresolved. The Arminians were Protestants who favoured a greater emphasis on ritual, set prayers, ceremony and reverence in church services. Also termed 'high church', this movement believed that religious affairs were best enforced by a strict episcopal system (a hierarchy of bishops and archbishops: see Figure 1.2). In order to counter the growth of Puritanism, Laud acted to restrict their preachers. He did this in two ways. First, he restricted preaching to Sunday mornings and evenings only, thus preventing the spontaneous sermons often given by Puritan clergy and lay preachers. Second, he banned an organisation known as the Feoffees for Impropriations and the clergy they supported were replaced by Arminians. This was a Puritan organisation that raised money to support the appointment of Puritan clergy and lecturers in the parishes. In 1633 Laud banned the Feoffees and the clergy they supported were replaced by Arminians. The attack on Puritans was extended to their general outlook and lifestyle. In 1633 Laud reissued the *Book of Sports*. Originally published in 1618 to encourage the population to partake in popular sports after Sunday church services. This was an affront to Puritans who felt that Sunday should be devoted to Bible reading and prayer.

One of the most important of Laud's reforms was the movement of the altar or communion table from the centre of a church, where it was surrounded by the laity (the people), to the most holy part of the church at the east end. New altar rails were put in place behind which only the clergy could go. Their importance was reinforced by

### Key term

**layperson:** someone who conducts or takes part in a religious service but is not officially ordained as a member of the clergy.

### Key term

**zealous:** used to describe the actions of someone who fervently believes in a cause, often at the expense of other interests. Someone who acted zealously would be called a zealot.

Diane Purkiss on people's concerns

If there was simmering discontent in the 1630s, it was not so much with Ship Money as with Archbishop Laud … So from a Godly point of view, the Church of England was being run by an emissary of hell, and the king was doing nothing to stop him. People began to wonder if Charles's Personal Rule risked running the kingdom into the arms of Rome.[5]

According to Diane Purkiss, what was the biggest impact of the Personal Rule and why?

the introduction of clerical robes, the instruction to bow at the name of Jesus and the use of the sign of the cross at baptisms, all very reminiscent of Catholicism.

Ceremony and order was encouraged through the use of the new **Book of Common Prayer** and the decoration of churches with stained glass and religious paintings. All of this was made possible by the appointment of Arminians to key bishoprics and the universities of Oxford and Cambridge, where the clergy were educated and where new scholarships were offered to Arminians. The episcopal system disseminated these reforms and the Church Courts, supported by prerogative courts like Star Chamber (see the section on Methods of government), enforced them. The whole system was further supported by bishops' 'visitations' to the parishes to check that Laudian reforms were being obeyed. The reforms certainly seem to have chimed with Charles's belief in the 'beauty of holiness' and his desire to achieve greater uniformity across his realm.

In 1637 a Scottish version of the Book of Common Prayer was produced in the hope that Charles's Presbyterian subjects would be brought into line. Resented by Scottish Presbyterians as an imposition, the whole process had been initiated by royal prerogative without any formal agreement or negotiation with the General Assembly of the Kirk. Alongside the Book of Common Prayer, Charles imposed new canons that ordered the altar to be placed at the east end of the church. Again, without consultation, this was a major affront to the Presbyterian congregations who operated a more communal style of worship in which ceremony played little part. A violent response was not long in coming.

## The growth of opposition from Puritans

For some of Charles's subjects, the Laudian reforms were acceptable. The decline of the established Church was something that was easy for all to see and in Laud's view the Church of England had been allowed to drift into a state of physical and moral decay, with the communion table becoming nothing more than a hat stand under which dogs could play, or as Laud complained, 'piss'.[6] But what he and Charles failed to appreciate was the reaction that these changes would evoke among those on the outer fringes of the religious spectrum, as well as some in the middle ground.

**Key term**

**Book of Common Prayer:** devised and enforced by the episcopal system of archbishops and bishops, the Book of Common Prayer provided a means by which religious worship was controlled. The book laid out orders of service and set prayers that the parish clergy were instructed to follow. High-church Anglicans saw the Book of Common Prayer as an important defence against the innovation of Puritan sermons.

## ACTIVITY 2.7

Summarise the beliefs of Puritans. How did they differ from mainstream Protestants?

**Figure 2.2:** Puritan woodcut, *Of God, Of Man, Of the Divell.* The Puritan minister on the left wears simple vestments and holds the Bible written in English, while at the other end of the spectrum the minister wears elaborate robes and carries a Latin book of set prayers.

Indeed, the reaction was strongest among the Puritans. To them Laudianism resembled Catholicism and was a threat to the Protestant Reformation. Laud's insistence that the word of God was best communicated by a priest from the pulpit undermined the Puritan emphasis on sermons preached by God's elect, whether layman or priest. Figure 2.2 shows the suspicion levelled at the archbishop's reforms by Puritans. Most high profile among the Puritan critics were the three gentlemen pamphleteers, Burton, Bastwick and Prynne, all of whom were convicted in 1637 by the Court of Star Chamber for defying Laud's censorship and publishing stinging criticism of the reforms. Prynne was already known to the authorities, having been punished in 1634 for an earlier pamphlet entitled *Histriomastrix*, which had attacked the Court and implied that the Queen was a whore. People were shocked by the brutality of their punishment, especially given their social rank as gentlemen. All three were imprisoned for life, fined £5000 each and publicly mutilated by having their ears 'clipped'. Prynne had already lost the top of his ears by way of punishment for his previous offence, but now had what was left of the stumps cut off and his cheeks branded.

**ACTIVITY 2.8**

Write a paragraph summarising the reasons why Laud's reforms of the Church were met with hostility.

**Figure 2.3:** This woodcut satirises the extreme nature of Laud's actions as Archbishop of Canterbury. The two gentlemen either side of him gesture at their clipped ears, which are being served as a meal for Laud. On the right, two priests hold muskets, inferring that Laud's reforms were carried out with force.

Concern was even felt by many mainstream Anglicans. As Blair Worden has commented, 'Among the laity, even non-Puritans were alarmed by Laud's clericalism and were puzzled by the king's support for it.'[7] It was this suspicion, deeply rooted in the English people's willingness to defend the achievements of the Reformation that gave Puritan opposition a weight beyond its numbers. While many leading Puritans chose to migrate to the 'howling wilderness' of the colonies in New England, others began to rally around political leaders like the Earl of Bedford, Viscount Saye and Sele and John Pym who would lead the assault on Laud and his policies in 1640.[8] As John Morrill has concluded: 'It is almost impossible to underestimate the damage caused by the Laudians … [Critics] found in Charles I a negligent king who was oblivious to the threat of popery at home, abroad, and within the church of which he was supreme governor.'[9]

🗨 **Voices from the past**

## Harbottle Grimstone

Harbottle Grimstone, a commoner, expressed his view of Archbishop Laud:

… the sty of pestilential filth that hath infested the state and government of this commonwealth … like a busie angry wasp, his sting is in the tayl of everything.[10]

# Political issues

## The role of Wentworth

As Laud unveiled religious reform, it was Wentworth who strove to enforce political obedience. He became symbolic of the authoritarian nature of Charles's Personal Rule. When Parliament was finally recalled in 1640, Wentworth, along with Laud, became the initial target of criticism. Hostile MPs readily accused Wentworth of playing the role of 'evil advisor' to the King. These attacks were fuelled by the fact many saw Wentworth as having betrayed his parliamentary colleagues in favour of promotion.

## Policies in Ireland and England

Wentworth's first appointment was as President of the Council of the North. He stated that 'the authority of a King is the keystone which closeth up the arch of order and government'.[12] At the heart of Wentworth's approach to government lay a belief that it should be 'thorough'. The term 'thorough government' was a phrase that Wentworth and Laud used in their letters to one another and in many ways came to epitomise Wentworth's methods. The policy of 'thorough' demanded that all officials should be held to account for their actions and inefficiency eradicated. He was particularly determined to impose conformity to the *Book of Orders* that had been issued in 1631. This required local officials like JPs and sheriffs to submit regular reports to central government. Similarly, Wentworth tried to improve county militias by ensuring they kept stores of gunpowder and ammunition, drilled regularly and were inspected by new commissioners.

Wentworth's appointment as Lord President of the Council of the North saw him put his policy of 'thorough' into operation with ruthless efficiency. Local officials were called before the Council to account for their actions and replaced if found wanting. The Council soon began to operate as a prerogative court like the Star Chamber, dispensing judgements and rulings outside the normal remit of the law. The northern gentry and nobles found themselves being disciplined, while the common people found themselves increasingly under authoritarian surveillance. Such a firm hand did bring efficiency and order but its abrupt nature did much to conjure up the feeling that England was becoming more like the absolute monarchies of mainland Europe.

In 1632, Wentworth's efficiency gained him promotion to the post of Lord Deputy of Ireland and unlike many of his predecessors Wentworth was successful in bringing Ireland under control. One of his greatest achievements was extracting £80 000 a year in subsidies from the Irish Parliament. In achieving this Wentworth ensured that Ireland ceased to be the financial drain on England that it had previously been. This was not, however, achieved through popular consent. Rather, Wentworth played rival groups off against each other, abandoning them after gaining what he needed. Indeed, Wentworth's approach to the Irish was harsh. In 1634 he brusquely refused to acknowledge a set of agreements called the 'graces', made by his predecessor, Lord Falkland. The graces, among other things, had sought to legalise land titles granted over the previous 60 years. In refusing to pass these into law, Wentworth was in a position to remove grants of land whenever he felt the need. Although this could be seen as a clever move on his part, it produced great hostility to English rule.

In a further step to cement English overlordship, Wentworth continued to develop the Protestant **plantations** used by previous monarchs. By encouraging movement of loyal English and Scottish Protestants to Ireland Wentworth ensured he had a natural support base; but his reasoning was more cunning than this, for he was also in a position to place them under heavier taxation, confident that they would not rebel. Any opposition that did emerge was dealt with brutally and imprisonment without charge was not unknown. As in England, prerogative courts were used such as the

**Speak like a historian: David Smith**

David Smith describes Wentworth as a formidable, but divisive figure in Charles's government:

'Although he had been one of the most outspoken critics of Buckingham and the policies of the 1620s, Wentworth had long sought to secure a foothold at Court, and from 1628 he proved himself a loyal servant of the Crown as President of the Council of the North. A blunt, ambitious and energetic Yorkshireman, he possessed a forceful personality, outstanding administrative ability and considerable political skill. His principal weaknesses were a lack of subtlety and tact, a tendency to oversimplify and a total incapacity either to compromise or to understand alternative points of view.'[11]

Court of High Commission and the Court of Castle Chamber. These courts sidestepped Common Law and helped build Wentworth's image as an enforcer of tyrannical rule.

On the religious front, Wentworth's governorship in Ireland sought to impose the Laudian reforms enacted in England. For once, the focus of English policy in Ireland did not concentrate on persecuting Irish Catholics. Instead, the imposition of the Thirty-Nine Articles in 1634 pressed Protestants to conform to the new methods of worship. As with their counterparts in England, the whiff of popery that accompanied the changes raised fears among Protestants in Ireland. In a letter to Laud, Wentworth described the reluctance of Irish Protestants to conform to the order to bow at the name of Christ: 'As for bowing at the name of Jesus, it will not down with them yet; they have no more joints in their knees for that than an elephant.'[13]

## The reactions against the Crown

One of the most significant impacts of Wentworth's rule in Ireland was the fact that he inadvertently united hostile groups. His high-handed tactics made it clear that English rule was intended for the benefit of the English monarch, not the Irish people. This shocked two previously hostile groups. On the one side there were the 'Old Irish' (the native Irish families who followed the Catholic faith, often referred to as Gaelic) and on the other the 'Old English' (settlers who had been in Ireland for generations and who were also Catholic). In failing to legalise their land holdings, Wentworth ensured these groups slowly grew together in opposition to the Crown. In addition, those on whom the English relied, the 'New English' (recent Protestant settlers) were themselves thrown into a state of insecurity. In their minds they were now trapped between the native Catholic Irish and the creeping popery of the Arminian reforms. In fear, they called for ever-harsher treatment of the Catholics and when Wentworth eventually left Ireland to help Charles deal with the troublesome Scots in 1639, the Catholic Irish saw their chance to avoid such harsh measures. In the autumn of 1641 they launched a ferocious rebellion, the legacy of which lasted for years to come. It put Charles under increasing pressure to secure subsidies from Parliament, raised fears of Catholic conspiracy and goes some way to explain the violence of Cromwell's Irish campaign in 1649–50.

In England, discontent with the Personal Rule remained largely muted. Wentworth's actions had given people a taste of authoritarian rule and few seemed to like it. Yet most conformed and complied with the demands placed on them. The old relationship between central and local government that had previously been a light-touch business, in which the local elites were given considerable freedom to run affairs as they saw fit, had been challenged. But by adopting methods that amounted

ACTIVITY 2.9

Why was the hostility towards Wentworth different from that levelled at Laud?

---

🔑 **Key term**

**plantations:** settlements of English and Scottish Protestants in Ireland.

---

to absolutism, the Personal Rule sharpened people's fears for the safety of the ancient constitution.

As we have seen, these political fears were shown in the hostility to the financial policies of the Crown. Yet despite the Hampden case, most people once again seem to have complied with the demands made of them. Nonetheless, what irked so many people was the precedent that was being set – taxation without parliamentary approval. This raised fears that royal powers and prerogatives were being expanded at the expense of Parliament's power over finance.

Lastly, the pattern of muffled opposition was repeated with the religious reforms. While some, like the parishioners of St Gregory's Church, near St Paul's Cathedral in London, unsuccessfully challenged the removal of their communion table to the east end of the church, the vast majority of congregations followed Laud's edicts. In a few cases the reforms may have been welcomed; however, to many the outpouring of hostility to Laud in the Parliaments of 1640 prove that while people conformed, many were deeply angered. Many no doubt shared the Earl of Bedford's belief that Laud was 'the little thief put into the window of the church to unlock the door to popery'.[14] Less exalted figures agreed. The headmaster of Westminster School, referring to Laud as he might have done one of his students, described him as a 'meddling little hocus-pocus'.[15] What is more, the enforcement of the Arminian reforms by Church and prerogative courts not only split religious opinion but once again raised fears of absolutism.

In short, reactions against the Crown were muted. However, the hostility that was growing below the surface was proved by the venom with which grievances finally poured forth against the 'evil advisors' when Parliament reassembled in 1640.

## Demands for the recall of Parliament

And so it was that the need for change began to dominate many people's thinking. This was most apparent in Scotland. Charles had treated his northern kingdom with disregard, leaving it to his Scottish Privy Councillors to enact royal decrees as best they could. Charles was suspicious of their Presbyterian national church and did little to gain favour with the Scottish nobility. In 1633, when he eventually visited Scotland for his formal coronation, he offended the Scots by adopting elements from the English coronation service. Given Wentworth's tactics in Ireland, it is unsurprising that many in England saw it as a frightening experiment in absolute royal power. The extension of Ship Money raised fears that Charles was creating a means by which he could rule without recourse to Parliament, while Laud's reforms of the Church raised fears of what a monarch could do when free from the advice of Parliament. Yet, for all these worries, the British Isles were at peace, the King balanced the books and churches echoed with the sound of tools constructing altar rails. No opportunity presented itself to demand the recall of Parliament until 1637 when events in Scotland gave critics a chance to make their voices heard.

## Radicalism, dissent and the approach of war

The Protestant Church in Scotland, or **Kirk** as it was known, followed the Presbyterian system. Holy communion was a simple, communal affair, in which the taking of bread and wine took place at long tables – a collective commemoration of Christ's sacrifice. In some ways Scottish services were similar to the style of worship preferred by Puritans in England. Preaching sermons and spontaneous prayer were the hallmark of the Presbyterian Kirk and control rested firmly at the parish level; communities elected representatives to sit in local councils and ultimately a national assembly. This 'bottom-up' form of organisation was in stark contrast to the 'top-down' episcopal system of bishops used to control the Church of England (see Figure 1.2). James had largely let the Kirk exist unaltered, satisfied that his native Scotland had accepted the introduction of bishops. For Charles, however, more needed to be done to bring his two kingdoms together. Thus, in October 1636, his Scottish Privy Council issued orders that services should be conducted using the new Scottish version of the Book of Common Prayer that had been introduced in England in 1633. The book immediately aroused Scottish fears that some ungodly plot was afoot to crush the Kirk of God's chosen people.

## The spread of religious radicalism

Matters came to a head in July 1637 at St Giles's Kirk, Edinburgh. Accompanied by the Scottish bishops and archbishops, the Dean began to read from the new Book of Common Prayer, only to be met with howls of objection and a hail of footstools thrown by women in the congregation. The chaos forced one of the bishops to abandon the set prayers and deliver a sermon instead. Outside the riot continued and when they left, the bishops were pelted with stones. As news spread, petitions flooded in, complaining about the new **Prayer Book** and urging the King to save his people from the innovations of the bishops. The King was unmoved and claimed authorship for himself, hoping in vain that this personal appeal would quell the growing furore. South of the border, the actions of the Scots aroused sympathy among their Protestant brothers. Despite tight controls on publications, attacks on the bishops and Laud's reforms began to circulate.

> ## Key term
>
> **Kirk:** the term for the Scottish Church.

> ## Key term
>
> **Prayer Book:** also called the English Book of Common Prayer. Devised and enforced by the episcopal system of Archbishops and Bishops, the Book of Common Prayer provided a means by which religious worship was controlled. The book laid out orders of service and set prayers that the Parish clergy were instructed to follow. High-Church Anglicans saw the Book of Common Prayer as an important defence against the innovation of Puritan sermons.

**Figure 2.4:** The riot at St Giles's Kirk, Edinburgh, and the attack on Laud's palace at Lambeth by the London Apprentices.

**ACTIVITY 2.10**

Why would the use of the Book of Common Prayer cause Scots to react in such a violent manner?

### Key term

**Covenanter:** those who signed the covenant (agreement) to defend the Scottish Presbyterian system. As a result it was used to describe the Scottish troops raised to fight first in the Bishops' Wars and in the civil wars that followed.

## The Scottish National Covenant and the First Bishops' War

Opposition to the Prayer Book was shown most clearly in the mass signing of the National Covenant in February 1638. This document, a collective declaration to defend the Presbyterian Church against popery and superstition, was signed by the majority of Scotland's nobility and ministers. In asserting their willingness to fight in defence of the Scottish Kirk, the **'Covenanters'**, careful to point out their loyalty to the Crown, did not wish to be seen as rebels but rather as loyal subjects, appealing to their Scottish King. This was a powerful claim that swayed many moderates in Scotland. It did not, however, sway Charles.

Charles first opened negotiations with the Covenanters by sending the Marquis of Hamilton, a trusted Scot, to treat with them. Hamilton was permitted to make some serious concessions, notably the withdrawal of the Book of Common Prayer. He also allowed the calling of a Scottish Parliament and a General Assembly of the Scottish Church. Much to Charles's annoyance, their first act was to abolish the episcopal system of bishops in Scotland. This antagonistic move was met with Charles's second strategy: military force. As England's inefficient militias began to creak into readiness for war, the King's double strategy only served to raise suspicions of his dishonesty.

## The Pacification of Berwick

In fact, suspicion of Charles's duplicity was well founded and Charles himself confided to Hamilton that concessions were only intended 'to win time … until I be ready to suppress them'.[17] Charles immediately began to raise **coat and conduct money** to finance the coming conflict. This was met with widespread disapproval and for the first time people began in large numbers to refuse to pay ship money. Not since 1323 had an English monarch gone to war without calling a parliament to provide supplies. Months passed as an army of ill-disciplined militia slowly amassed and made its way north.

The Scottish army was far superior to the English force, which they met at Kelso, near Berwick, in June 1639. By this time, the inexperienced English troops were so demoralised that their commanders immediately sued for peace without having even fired a shot. This abortive conflict, known as the First Bishops' War, was ended by the Pacification of Berwick, an agreement whereby Charles agreed to the calling

### Hidden voices

#### *Contemporary posters and broadsheets*

These give us a glimpse of what the illiterate classes were thinking. Written texts, songs and verse would often be read or performed to a crowd. The following verse was published in London in 1639. It clearly shows sympathy for the Scottish cause and the hope that the King would give in:

**O yes, o yes, I do cry, the bishops' bridles will you buy**
Since bishops first began to ride
in state, so near the crown,
they have been aye puffed up with pride,
and rode with great renown;
but GOD hath pulled these prelates down,

in spite of Spain and pope;
so shall their next eclipse be soon
in England seen I hope …

So let the devil go bishop them,
as he hath done before,
for never man shall worship them
in any kingdom more:
for Scotland that they crossed so sore,
shall now with gladness sing,
and bless him did our state restore,
that was our gracious king.[16]

of another Scottish Parliament and General Assembly. Satisfied that their actions had secured a peaceful resolution to the crisis, these bodies immediately ratified the abolition of bishops in Scotland. To Charles, however, the fight was far from over, and the Pacification of Berwick was merely a breathing space before he renewed his attack.

## The Second Bishops' War

While the Covenanters were happy with their successes, they must have known that in time the greater resources of England would see their military defeat. Thus it was that they began actively to evoke sympathy for their cause amongst those in England who were equally dissatisfied with Laud's reforms. Just as the Scottish Parliament passed a Triennial Act, ensuring it would be called every three years, contacts were being made with leading politicians in England. Confident that they would receive their support, the Scots began to call for an English Parliament.

Wentworth, newly returned from Ireland and created Earl of Strafford, argued that summoning Parliament was not an act of weakness. Rather, it could be trusted to act on its historic anti-Scottish feeling and grant funds for a second war against the rebellious Scots. Persuaded by Wentworth's arguments, Charles agreed and in April 1640 what became known as the Short Parliament assembled.

The concerns and fears that had built up during the Personal Rule were immediately vented. The majority of MPs and some Lords believed that their religious, legal and constitutional grievances should be resolved before any subsidies were granted to the King. In using their control of taxation, the Short Parliament had effectively created deadlock. It sat for a mere three weeks before Charles dissolved it, urged on by Wentworth's belief that he was now 'loose and absolved from all rules of government'.[19] Wentworth went so far as to suggest that the King should bring an army from Ireland to suppress his opponents and secured a subsidy from the Irish Parliament to support the campaign. This action would later cost Wentworth his life. In dissolving the Short Parliament Charles strengthened the hostility of the Scottish Covenanters and those in England who sympathised with their position. Their growing mistrust was made worse by Charles's decision to allow the **Convocation of the Clergy**, normally dissolved with Parliament, to continue sitting. This body granted Charles a £20 000 subsidy and in May 1640, at the King's instruction, it issued 17 new canons (religious laws). This inevitably fuelled fears that Charles was seeking to raise funds without parliamentary consent and that he was bent on embedding the Laudian reforms. Most significant was the canon that required the clergy to swear the 'Et Cetera Oath' – an oath that safeguarded the system of bishops.

In August 1640 Charles cobbled together another army to confront the Scots, who stole the initiative and invaded England, determined now to confront the threat to the 'true religion' of both kingdoms. The widespread support for the Covenanters was revealed in the actions of Charles's own troops, many of whom assaulted officers they suspected of being Catholic, committed **iconoclasm** in churches, and in some cases mutinied outright. This was no shirking on their part, but rather the actions of religiously and politically aware individuals. Whatever their motive, it undermined Charles's military force, and on 28 August the Covenanters routed the English army at the battle of Newburn and occupied the northeast of England, besieging Newcastle.

Having failed militarily for a second time, 12 English nobles petitioned Charles to recall Parliament and redress the nation's grievances. Some of these nobles were certainly in communication with their Scottish counterparts, and had their correspondence been discovered, they would have been exposed to the charge of treason. However, Charles was now trapped. After the defeat at Newburn the King was forced to sign the Treaty of Ripon with the Scots, agreeing to pay £850 a day for the maintenance of the Scottish army until a satisfactory peace could be concluded. Charles, having gathered a Great

### Key term

**Convocation of the Clergy:** the formal meeting of the clergy of the Church of England. The Convocation operated much like a parliament, making decisions on Church rules and doctrine. It was called whenever a Parliament was called and traditionally came to an end whenever Parliament was dissolved. In 1640 it continued to sit despite the fact that the Short Parliament had been dissolved by Charles I.

### Key term

**iconoclasm:** the destruction religious icons, images and symbols, such as stained glass and statues.

## ACTIVITY 2.11

Create a timeline of events for the period 1637–40. Note key events and identify the moments when:

1. Charles lost control of the situation
2. Charles could have achieved a peaceful settlement of the crisis
3. Charles had no choice but to recall Parliament.

Council of Nobles at York, was now under unprecedented political and financial pressure, and so acquiesced to their wish. The Long Parliament assembled in London on 3 November 1640.

### Further reading

Coverage of this period from the perspective of people who lived through the events can be found in Purkiss D. *The English Civil War: A People's History*. London: Harper Perennial; 2007. A good summary of the course of events can be gained from Worden B. *The English Civil Wars, 1640–1660*. London: Weidenfeld and Nicholson; 2009. A more detailed narrative is given in Braddick M. *God's Fury, England's Fire: A New History of the English Civil Wars*. London: Penguin; 2009.

### Taking it further

Some historians, such as Christopher Hill, have suggested that the Short and Long Parliaments represented a degree of class tension. Research Christopher Hill's Marxist viewpoint and examine his argument using the knowledge you have gained in this chapter. Was this really a class war? A good starting point would be Chapter 2 of Hill's book *The World Turned Upside Down*.[18]

### Practice essay questions

1. 'Religious reforms were the biggest source of discontent during the Personal Rule.' Explain why you agree or disagree with this view.
2. 'Charles managed to rule successfully and without much opposition, 1629–40.' Explain why you agree or disagree with this view.
3. 'The Scottish rejection of the Prayer Book was the most significant reason the Personal Rule came to an end.' Assess the validity of this view.
4. With reference to these extracts and your understanding of the historical context, which of these two sources is more valuable for explaining the problems brought about by Charles's Personal Rule?

**Extract A**

The Venetian Ambassador's report to his government on John Hampden's case, 1637

Your Excellencies can easily understand the great consequences involved in this decision [that of the judges in favour of ship money], as at one stroke it roots out forever the meeting of Parliament and renders the King absolute and sovereign. It has created such consternation and disorder that one cannot judge what the outcome will be. If the people submit to this present prejudice, they are submitting to an eternal yoke … thus finally the goal will be reached for which the King has been labouring so long.[20]

**Extract B**

The official record of the protest of a London Parish, January 1640.

Some of the parishioners of the parish of Allhallows Barking London lately exhibited a petition unto the right honourable and right reverend father in God William [Juxon] lord bishop of London setting forth that of late years the said parish church hath been repaired and beautified and a new font erected and the communion table placed and railed about according to the laws, canons and customs of the Church of England and that over the font is set or placed certain carved images, the picture of the Holy Ghost, and a cross. And that also the communion table is removed out of its ancient and accustomed place, and certain images placed on the rail that standeth round about it, which images they desire to be taken down, and the communion table set in the place where it formerly stood.[21]

## Chapter summary

By the end of this chapter you should have gained a broad overview of Charles I's attempts to rule without a Parliament and the pressures he faced towards the end of the Personal Rule. The impact of his religious policies in provoking a response, particularly in Scotland, should be especially apparent. In particular you should be able to:

- explain the methods that Charles used to run his kingdoms in the 1630s
- give examples of successes and failures of the Personal Rule
- describe the extent of opposition provoked by the Personal Rule
- explain the significance of Laud's reforms in causing a crisis in Scotland
- explain why Charles I was forced to recall Parliament in 1640.

## End notes

1  Sharpe K. *Stuart Monarchy and Political Culture*. In Morrill J. (ed.) *The Oxford Illustrated History of Tudor and Stuart Britain*. Oxford: OUP; 2000. p. 249.

2  Quoted in Gardiner SR. (ed.) *The Constitutional Documents of the Puritan Revolution 1625–1660*. Oxford: OUP; 1889. p. 31.

3  For the figure raised by Distraint of Knighthood, see Braddick M. *God's Fury, England's Fire: A New History of the English Civil Wars*. London: Penguin Books; 2009. p. 68.

4  Braddick M. *God's Fury, England's Fire: A New History of the English Civil Wars*. London: Penguin Books; 2009. p. 70.

5  Purkiss D. *The English Civil War. London: Harper Perennial; 2007.* p. 26.

6  Quoted in Durston C. *Charles I*. London: Routledge; 1998. p. 164.

7  Worden B. *The English Civil Wars, 1640–1660*. London: Weidenfeld and Nicholson; 2009. p. 23.

8  Hughes A. *The Causes of the English Civil War*. London: Palgrave Macmillan; 1998. p. 157.

9  John Morrill has argued convincingly that the impact of Laud cannot be underestimated. See Morrill J. *The Nature of the English Revolution*. London: Pearson Education; 1993. p. 52–54.

10  Quoted in Morrill J. *The Nature of the English Revolution*. p. 54.

11  Smith DL. *A History of the Modern British Isles, 1603–1707*. Oxford: OUP; 1998. p. 98.

12  Hibbert C. *Charles I*. p.140.

13  Quoted in Smith DL. *A History of the Modern British Isles, 1603–1707*. p. 99.

14  Quoted in Smith DL. *A History of the Modern British Isles, 1603–1707*. p. 95.

15  Quoted in Smith DL. *A History of the Modern British Isles, 1603–1707*. p. 98.

16  PRO, state papers, domestic 16/538/140 quoted in Lindley K. *The English Civil War and Revolution: A Sourcebook*. London: Routledge; 1998. p. 41–42.

17  Quoted in Smith DL. *A History of the Modern British Isles, 1603–1707*. p. 110.

18  Hill C. *The World Turned Upside Down: Radical Ideas During the English Revolution*. London: Penguin; 1991.

19  Quoted in Worden B. *The English Civil Wars, 1640–1660*. p. 29.

20  Braddick M. *God's Fury, England's Fire: A New History of the English Civil Wars*. London: Penguin Books; 2009. p. 99–103.

21  Quoted in Lindley K. *The English Civil War and Revolution: A Sourcebook*. London: Routledge; 1998. p. 39–40. Original source: Greater London Record Office, consistory court of London DL/C/344, ff.68-9 vicar-general's book.

# 3 The crisis of Parliament and the outbreak of the First Civil War, 1640–1642

In this section we will examine the crisis that emerged when Charles recalled Parliament. We will look into:

- The Political Nation 1640: the recall of Parliament; the strengths and weaknesses of Charles I; the strengths and divisions of parliamentary opposition.
- Pym and the development of parliamentary radicalism: Pym's personality and aims; the Grand Remonstrance; the London mob; popular radicalism.
- Conflicts between Crown and Parliament: attempts to impose royal authority and the development of a Royalist party; the execution of Strafford and its political consequences.
- The slide into war: the impact of events in Ireland; the failed arrest of the Five Members; local grievances; failure of negotiations between the King and the Long Parliament; military preparations for war.

## Introduction

In 1640 Charles I recalled Parliament after 11 years of Personal Rule. Rather than provide the King with the funds that he needed to deal with the Bishops' Wars with the Scots, MPs decided that their grievances should be dealt with first. Frustrated with their defiance and eager to pursue other forms of financial support, Charles dismissed this Short Parliament after a sitting of only three weeks. As the crisis continued to deepen it became apparent that Charles had no option than to call another Parliament to help provide him with the funds he required.

The new Parliament that assembled on 3 November 1640 remained in existence, in one form or another, until 1660 and consequently became nicknamed the Long Parliament. Yet, from the very start it was destined to play an important role in the decline of the British Isles into a long series of bloody civil wars. As they took their seats in Westminster, the MPs were united in their grievances against 11 years of royal abuses of power. Chief among their concerns were the raising of taxes without parliamentary consent and the Laudian reforms to the Church of England. In MPs' eyes, the former threatened to establish an absolutist monarchy, while the latter threatened the achievements of the English Reformation and the survival of English Protestantism. The stage was clearly set for a clash of wills that would ultimately lead to division and war.

## Timeline

| 1640 | **3 November:** Long Parliament assembles<br>**November:** Strafford imprisoned and impeachment articles drawn up<br>**18 December:** Laud impeached<br>**December:** Impeachment of judges who had upheld Ship Money |
|---|---|
| 1641 | **25 January:** Charles promises to defend 'the true Protestant religion by law established'<br>**8–9 February:** Commons debates London Root and Branch Petition<br>**15 February:** Triennial Act; Parliament to be summoned at least every three years<br>**9 May:** Death of Earl of Bedford: effectively ends attempts to create 'bridge-appointments'<br>**10 May:** Charles assents to Strafford's Attainder and to Bill against the dissolution of Parliament without its own consent<br>**12 May:** Strafford executed<br>**22 June:** abolition of tonnage and poundage<br>**5 July:** abolition of Prerogative Courts; judicial powers of Privy Council, Council in the North<br>**August:** Ship Money and knighthood fines declared illegal<br>**August:** Charles agrees settlement with Scots<br>**1 September:** Commons passes resolution for destruction of altar rails, candlesticks and crucifixes<br>**11–12 October:** Scottish 'Incident'<br>**October:** Irish Catholic rebellion; second Army Plot revealed<br>**22–23 November:** Commons narrowly passes Grand Remonstrance by 159 votes to 148<br>**21 December:** City of London elects a new Common Council much more sympathetic towards Pym and his allies<br>**23 December:** Charles rejects Grand Remonstrance<br>**27–30 December:** crowds prevent bishops from entering the Lords; bishops impeached |

| 1642 | **4 January:** Charles's attempted arrest of five MPs |
|---|---|
| | **10 January:** Charles and his family retreat to Hampton Court |
| | **23 February:** Henrietta Maria leaves England to raise money for troops |
| | **5 March:** Houses of Parliament pass the Militia Ordinance |
| | **2 June:** Houses of Parliament present the *Nineteen Propositions* to Charles which he rejects |
| | **11 June:** Charles issues commissions of array to raise troops |
| | **July:** Houses of Parliament vote to raise an army of 10 000 volunteers; Essex appointed Lord General |
| | **18 August:** Houses of Parliament declare Charles's supporters 'traitors' |
| | **22 August:** Charles raises standard at Nottingham |

## The Political Nation 1640

### The recall of Parliament

If Charles had hoped that the Long Parliament would be different in attitude to its predecessor, he was sorely disappointed. The MPs and Lords were confident that they had the initiative due to serious financial pressures. Charles had failed to win the Second Bishops' War and the resulting Treaty of Ripon ensured he had to pay £850 per day for the maintenance of the Scottish army that occupied the northeast of England. The MPs knew that the King's reliance on them for subsidies would give them a chance to seek redress for grievances that had built up during the Personal Rule. Among these were objections to Laud's religious reforms, non-parliamentary taxation and the role played by the King's advisors. Until these issues had been addressed, Parliament was in no mood to grant Charles the finances he needed. Nevertheless, there were many who hoped that resolution of their grievances would return the kingdom to normality. One MP, Sir Henry Slingsby, wrote: 'Great expectance there is of a happy Parliament where the subject may have a total redress of all his grievances.'[1]

### The strengths and weaknesses of Charles I

Although Charles saw parliamentary opposition as a personal affront to his authority, in reality, much of the anger was not levelled at Charles himself but at his advisors. This gave the King an important advantage. It should be remembered that the MPs and Lords who raised grievances in 1640 were not opposed to monarchy; while they were opposed to the Crown's policies, they were not **republicans**. On the contrary, many were eager to see Charles saved from the clutches of the 'evil councillors'[3] Laud and Wentworth. The distinction between the King and his ministers was important because it gave many MPs the confidence to attack the abuses of the Personal Rule while avoiding personal criticism of Charles. In their eyes, they were simply restoring the balance between Crown and Parliament embodied in England's ancient constitution. Even radical opponents like Pym argued that his opposition to Laud and Wentworth did not mean he wished to demean the King himself (see Voices from the past: John Pym). In drawing upon people's traditional reverence for the office of king, Charles in theory could have enjoyed the support of many moderate MPs and Lords who were fearful of radical change.

Another of Charles's strengths was his willingness to compromise on certain matters. Although Charles was by nature stubborn, it became clear in 1640–41 that he was to some degree willing to give way when placed under pressure. During the first year of the Long Parliament Charles gave way over a number of important issues, including the Triennial Act (an agreement to call a parliament at least every third year), the 'Own Consent' Act (a law that meant Parliament could only be dissolved with its own consent), the removal of Laud and Wentworth, the ending of Ship Money and the reversal of many of Laud's Arminian reforms (see the section on The strengths and

### ACTIVITY 3.1

Read Baxter's account of the Long Parliament, which appears in the centre of Figure 3.1. Link the boxes that surround the extract to relevant points in the text.

### Key term

**republicans:** people who oppose monarchy or monarchical forms of government.

The Court of Star Chamber (and other prerogative courts) was under direct control of the monarch and was used to impose fines on those unwilling to conform to Charles's reforms. It operated in secret and it was perceived as an unjust 'private' court bent to the King's will.

The introduction of Arminianism by Laud in Church doctrine alienated Puritans. It also spread fear amongst mainstream Protestants who feared a return to more high-church or Catholic worship.

There was common dislike for Thomas Wentworth, Earl of Strafford (one of Charles's advisors) as a repressive figure and a destroyer of English liberty. His hard-line actions in Ireland supported this view.

In 1637 three leading Puritan gentleman, Burton, Prynne and Bastwick faced trial before Court of Star chamber. They were mutilated, pilloried and imprisoned for attacking the bishops. That this should be done to gentlemen was unheard of. They became martyrs to the anti-Laudian cause.

They made many long and vehement speeches against the Ship Money and against the judges that gave their judgement for it, and against the Et Cetera oath (a promise to obey all the new rules of the Church) and the bishops and convocation that were the formers of it; but especially against the Lord Thomas Wentworth, Lord Deputy of Ireland, and Dr Laud, Archbishop of Canterbury, as evil councillors, the cause of all.

*(By Richard Baxter, a Puritan Minister describing the mood of the Commons in 1640)*

Many believed that settlement with the King could still be achieved. There was no open desire for a republic, and no one at this point was challenging the institution of monarchy. People hoped that the grievances of Parliament would be addressed.

With a lack of parliamentary supplies Charles had been forced to rely on Ship Money, even extending it to inland shires. In the infamous case in 1637 John Hampton refused to pay Ship Money, and although he lost the case, he came to represent gentry opposition to arbitrary rule.

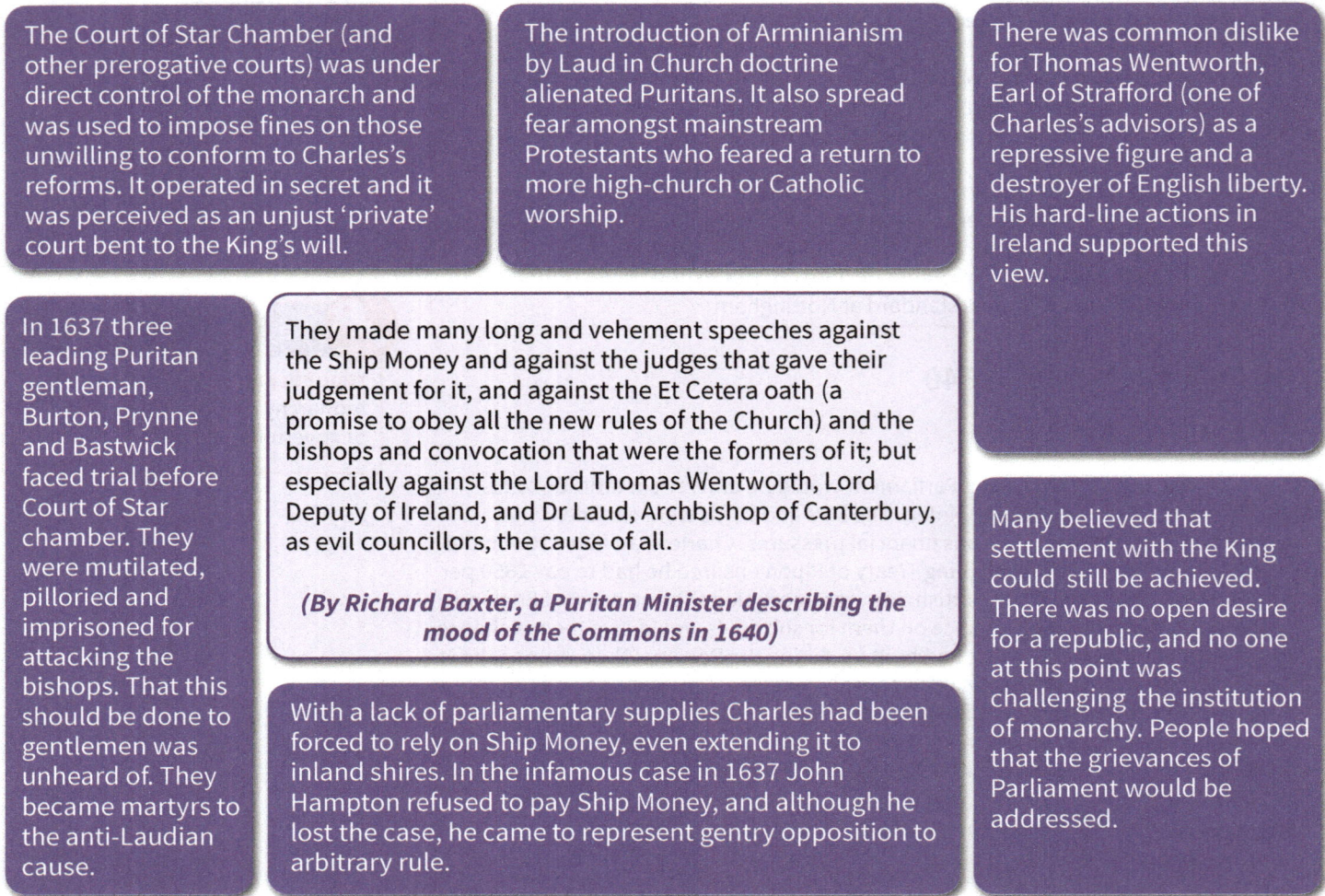

**Figure 3.1:** The preoccupations of MPs during the Long Parliament.[2]

## ACTIVITY 3.2

Why did MPs feel confident in attacking the Personal Rule?

divisions of parliamentary opposition). Again, in theory, such actions on Charles's part could have appeared reasonable and gained him support. However, Charles failed to capitalise on these potential strengths because he failed to gain the trust of moderate MPs. In the period 1640–42, three events did more than any other to damage the King's reputation.

The first two were termed the Army Plots. As Wentworth's trial proceeded between March and May 1641, some of the King's supporters, including Lord Goring, proposed moving the army south to London to suppress political opposition. There was also word of a royalist attempt to seize the Tower of London and free Wentworth from

### Voices from the past

#### John Pym

John Pym's speech to the House of Commons, 7 November 1640

[There is] a design to alter the kingdom both in religion and government. This is the highest of treason, this blows up by piecemeal, and almost goeth through [to] their ends. This concerns the king as well as we, and that I say with reverence and care of his Majesty.[4]

captivity. The King did little to distance himself from the plot (sometimes referred to as the Ashburnham Plot after one of the officers involved). The failure of the first plot was soon followed by a second hatched in June 1641 and revealed to Parliament in October. Once again, it seemed as though the King was willing to use military force to purge Parliament of its ringleaders. Significantly, these plots alienated many moderate MPs from the King, stiffened resistance to royal policies and gave Pym the confidence to push for further redress of grievances.

A similar story was played out in Scotland in an event simply referred to as the 'Incident'. By August 1641 Charles had managed to negotiate a withdrawal of the Scottish army in exchange for concessions that he was unwilling to grant in England – notably, the abolition of bishops. Sympathy for the King was beginning to emerge among some Scottish nobles yet the King managed to get himself involved in a bungled attempt to murder leading Covenanters like the Duke of Argyll and Lord Hamilton.

## The strengths and divisions of parliamentary opposition

If the King's position was weakened by his own actions, then the position of his opponents in Parliament was certainly strengthened by them. This strength was further increased by the unity of MPs over their desire to challenge the abuses of the Personal Rule. In an age before political parties, when parliaments were normally divided into loose and ever-changing factions and groups, it was remarkable that there was such unanimous pressure for reform. With the support of MPs who would later become royalists, this pressure bore fruit. As soon as Parliament assembled Wentworth and Laud were imprisoned and impeached and Laud's canons (religious laws issued earlier that year) were declared illegal. This was soon followed in February 1641 by the Triennial Act (ensuring a parliament at least every three years) and in March the trial of Wentworth began. Even when Wentworth successfully defended himself against the charge of treason, MPs were united enough to use an Act of Attainder to secure a guilty verdict without the need for evidence.

Yet below this façade of cooperation differing motives loomed. Moderate MPs and peers, like the future royalists Edward Hyde and Lord Falkland, were clearly motivated by a desire to confront the dubious legality of the Personal Rule. On the other hand, Pym and his Puritan followers in Parliament (Pym's junto, as they became known) were driven more by a desire to defeat a plot to alter the nation's religion. Yet, despite this division in aims, at this stage, they were united and the King could do little if they acted together.

By February 1641, after their first flush of success, weaknesses in the parliamentary opposition began to emerge over religion. With Laud successfully removed, the question of the future of the Church of England could not be ignored. On the one side, Pym's junto were urged on by their 'godly zeal' and fought eagerly for the abolition of bishops and a total reform of the Church. This attitude was revealed in their support for the Root and Branch Petition, which was hotly debated in Parliament on 8–9 February and which argued that the entire Church system should be amended along more Puritan lines. Opposed to these religious 'zealots' were more moderate MPs. They were happy to be rid of Laud and his authoritarian approach to Church government but they believed the episcopal system of bishops was sound (see Voices from the past: Lord Digby). It is important to note that the division of MPs in the debates over the Root and Branch Petition closely reflected people's future allegiance in the Civil War. Concerns for the future of England's Church were clearly becoming a divisive and motivating factor.

In other areas, however, unity was as strong as ever. In May 1641 both Houses voted unanimously in favour of the Protestation Oath, which committed MPs to oppose all forms of tyrannical government or attempts to undermine the 'true Protestant

---

### ACTIVITY 3.3

Read Pym's speech to the House of Commons in Voices from the past and then consider the following questions.

1. Whose 'design' is Pym referring to?

2. What does Pym's speech reveal about the nature of MPs' concerns in 1640 and their attitude to the King?

### ACTIVITY 3.4

Read the sections on The strengths and weaknesses of Charles I and The strengths and divisions of parliamentary opposition.

1. Draw up lists of the strengths and weaknesses of both the King and parliamentary opposition.

2. What did Parliament manage to achieve in 1640–41? Which was the most significant achievement and why?

> 💬 **Speak like a historian**
>
> ### *John Miller*
>
> A key focus of John Miller's research has been on power relations. Here he suggests that Charles I failed to build on the English willingness to accept royal authority.
>
> One of the monarchy's greatest assets was the willingness of the English to submit to royal authority and their expectation that the king should govern. Charles was temperamentally incapable of understanding this … Charles's seemingly wilful incomprehension drove essentially obedient subjects to make demands which they had not made of any of his predecessors.[5]

religion'. This unanimity was echoed a few days later when the Own Consent Act was passed ensuring that Parliament would need to give consent for its dissolution by the monarch. This erosion of the royal prerogative was grudgingly accepted by Charles, as were a whole raft of measures taken to ensure that a Personal Rule would be impossible in future. These included abolition of tonnage and poundage without parliamentary consent, the abolition of prerogative courts, and the removal of legal powers from the Privy Council. In addition, Ship Money was made illegal, knighthood fines were ended and forest fines limited. All the means by which the Personal Rule had been supported were now removed.

Yet, once again, cracks soon appeared between those in favour of more far-reaching changes to constitutional arrangements and moderates who felt that too much reform threatened the balance between Crown and Parliament. In this case, the major sticking-point was whether the King should be given a regular and guaranteed lump sum in place of parliamentary subsidies. In exchange, it was proposed that leading MPs, including Pym, would be given key positions as the King's ministers to keep him in check. However, fears that this would weaken Parliament's control of finances saw MPs divided over the issue and the proposal was not passed.

## Pym and the development of parliamentary radicalism

One of the leaders of parliamentary opposition to Charles's policies was John Pym, MP for Tavistock in Devon. He had entered political life through the patronage of the Earl of Bedford and was first elected MP in 1624. Pym had fought eagerly for the impeachment of the Duke of Buckingham and had strongly supported the Petition of Right presented to Charles I in 1628. During the Personal Rule Pym remained heavily involved in Puritan circles, serving as the treasurer for the Providence Island Company, which brought him into even closer contact with leading Puritan parliamentarians. He was well connected to other leading Puritans in both the Commons and the Lords.

### Pym's personality and aims

Having been educated in the law, Pym was able to argue and debate with intelligence and passion. He believed that assertive pressure was the best way to extract concessions from the King. At times his determination to achieve his aims led him to break the conventions of the time. He regularly appealed to the London mob for popular support on the streets, and also communicated with the Scots in what Charles would certainly have seen as an act of treason.

In his speeches in the Short Parliament Pym argued that England faced three threats. The first was the threat to the liberty of Parliament from royal absolutism, the second the threat to religion from popish influences and the third the threat to the law and rights of English people. In raising these issues Pym came to represent and unite many of the grievances that were raised by MPs in both the Short and Long Parliaments.

Pym's driving motivation was his stance on religious matters. This was shown in his vehement support for the Protestation Oath of May 1641, which was taken by MPs to defend 'the true reformed Protestant religion'. Pym went so far as to recommend it be extended throughout the whole nation in order to drive out popish plotters. He firmly supported the Root and Branch Petition and argued for the abolition of bishops. Indeed, throughout the sitting of the Long Parliament the printing presses regularly showed Pym to be the great defender against a series of popish plots (Figure 3.2). Yet, for all this, he could be a divisive figure too. This became apparent as the Long Parliament progressed and Pym lost the support of the moderate MPs who feared his attacks on the King's authority went too far.

## The Grand Remonstrance

As spring 1641 turned to summer, the King shifted his attention northwards to make a final settlement with the Scots. Resisting an attempt by Pym to control the appointment of his advisors, the King left the MPs to their debates. Departing for Scotland on 13 August, the King used what resources he had managed to gather to negotiate a withdrawal of the Scottish army from England. In exchange he made a series of concessions that he was not willing to make in England, notably the abolition of bishops in Scotland and appointments of Covenanters to government posts. While these far-reaching compromises gained Charles some goodwill in Scotland, his involvement in the 'Incident' robbed him of widespread support (see the section on The strengths and weaknesses of Charles I).

Nonetheless, in negotiating a settlement with the Scots, Charles had removed a major obstacle. The financial pressure that had necessitated the calling of the Long Parliament was now gone. In addition, discussions over religious reform were proving divisive among MPs and there was an increasing number that felt that enough had been achieved. By October, it finally seemed as though Charles might have been able to gain the support of enough MPs to bring discussions to an end and dissolve Parliament with its own consent.

Events, however, moved too fast for Charles to act and on 1 November 1641 the first reports reached London of a bloody and explosive rebellion in Ireland. The Catholic Irish, fearful of a Protestant crusade against them, had decided to strike first. Hundreds of Protestant landowners and clergy were killed, estates plundered and homes burned. Panic ensued and in England pamphleteers peddled rumours of numerous atrocities committed against Protestant kin in Ireland – tales abounded of massacres, robbery and murder, of babies ripped from their mothers' wombs and of Protestants stripped naked and sent to die of exposure in the hills. While the reports were exaggerated, the fear that gripped Parliament was real. Once again, the King required funds for an army and any chance of a dissolution of Parliament evaporated.

**ACTIVITY 3.5**

1. How could you use your knowledge of the King's actions in 1641 to support John Miller's argument?

2. What are the demands that John Miller argues were being made on Charles?

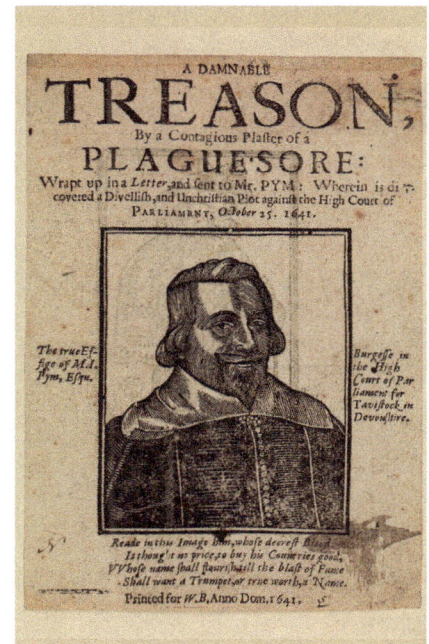

**Figure 3.2:** This pamphlet tells the story of 'a damnable treason', when a plaster infected with pus from a plague sore was sent to Pym in 1641. This attack was seen to be part of a Catholic plot against the nation.[7]

## Voices from the past

### Lord Digby

Lord Digby, a future royalist, spoke the following words in a debate on the Root and Branch Petition in 1641:

[It would be wrong] to root up a good tree because there is a canker in the branches … Let us not destroy bishops, but make bishops such as they were in primitive times.[6]

Debates in the Commons now centred on whether the King could be trusted with an army. The question of trust was made even more acute due to the fact that the rebels in Ireland claimed falsely that they had risen up by order of the King. Although this was pure invention, memories of the King's supposed involvement in the Army Plots haunted MPs and Pym moved that commanders of troops be agreed by Parliament. When this failed to gain unanimous support he went further and suggested that Parliament raise troops without the King's consent in order to quell the popish Irish rebels.

It was against this backdrop that Pym and his allies decided to recommence their campaign against the King and draw up a remonstrance that reminded people of the abuses of Charles's government since 1625. The Grand Remonstrance, as it was titled, also suggested a programme of reforms that would prevent personal rule, empower Parliament, and reform the Church in such a way that it would be free from Catholic influences. In many ways the Irish Rebellion spurred Pym on and justified what many saw as a personal attack on Charles. The lengthy content of the Grand Remonstrance, which contained 204 points in total, focused entirely on the ills experienced since Charles came to the throne in 1625.[8]

In stoking people's fears, and putting further demands on the King, the Remonstrance raised the stakes. This created a new phase of opposition that went well beyond the initial grievances raised in 1640–41 and continued to drive a wedge between two emerging sides. On the one hand there were those in support of Pym who were gripped by fears of a Catholic plot. On the other were those now sympathetic to the King and fearful that attacks on the royal prerogative were becoming almost treasonable in nature. After fierce debate, the Grand Remonstrance passed by the narrowest of margins: 159 votes to 148. Events now moved faster than participants expected as MPs decided that the Remonstrance should be circulated in print to the people of London and beyond. This was a breach of the normal protocol; the common people did not normally have any right to partake in political matters. That they were now engaged in the debate through the publication of the Remonstrance was a high-risk strategy on Pym's part. Seeing that pressure had worked in the past he may have hoped that the power of the London mob would convince the King to accept the document, but he was disappointed and on 23 December the King, insulted and outraged by the breach of normal conventions, rejected the Grand Remonstrance outright. For many contemporaries, things had unexpectedly gone too far and sympathy for the King grew (see Voices from the past: Edward Dering).

## The London mob

Although the 'political nation' was officially only made up of those men who owned sufficient property to give them a vote, the invention of the printing press in the previous century ensured that debate now reached the eyes and ears of the common people, especially in London.

Attacks on Laud's palace at Lambeth in 1640 and demonstrations on the streets of the capital (in favour of Strafford's trial, the Root and Branch Petition and the Grand

## Voices from the past

### *Edward Dering*

Edward Dering was MP for Kent and had supported the trial of Strafford and the restrictions on the power of bishops. By the end of 1642, however, he no longer felt comfortable with the development of events.

I did not dream that we should remonstrate downward, tell tales to the people, and talk of the king as a third person.[9]

Remonstrance) shocked the conservative-minded moderates within Parliament. As Purkiss has pointed out, they were 'alarmed by the coincidence of these demonstrations with Pym's assaults in the House of Commons, thinking that the radicals in Parliament were orchestrating the mobs'.[10]

Although it is unfair to suggest that Pym actively coordinated the London mob, he certainly understood the benefit of whipping up the apprentices in the capital. The apprentices were young men joined to a master in order to learn a trade. They had a strong group identity and were fiercely Protestant in outlook. Combining the radicalism of youthful disobedience with the zeal of religious conviction, their power was shown in demonstrations outside Parliament and the Palace of Whitehall during Wentworth's trial in May 1641. On this occasion they managed to intimidate the Lords sufficiently so that only a handful attended the final vote, ensuring that the Act of Attainder against Wentworth was passed by a majority of seven votes.[11] The mob then sealed Wentworth's fate on 10 May when the King, fearful for the safety of the royal family, gave his assent to the death warrant.

## Popular radicalism

The explosion of political activity among the population of London was not unique. It is easy for us to imagine that the people of England at this time were so removed from politics that they had little interest in the developing crisis. However, a century of religious reform and counter-reformation had so affected their lives that the people were highly engaged in political developments. Although primitive forms of communication slowed the spread of information, they also ensured that rumour and fears sharpened people's views.

Just as Parliament discussed the Root and Branch Petition, in the spring of 1641 many counties drew up their own petitions in favour of reform. Pen and paper often gave way to violence and spontaneous acts of iconoclasm. Taking the law into their own hands, mobs began smashing the stained glass windows of churches and ripping out altar rails. Basic law and order were disintegrating. Riots about **enclosure** erupted across the provinces as people challenged the fencing-in of land that had previously been available to the common people. In the eyes of the gentry the crisis was now threatening the very basis of everyday hierarchy and order.

The printing of pamphlets, newsletters and petitions both reflected and fed the growing crisis. The use of the written word alongside visual images and the culture of group reading meant the general public became truly engaged in the debate. The sheer number of printed pamphlets available was unprecedented, with one contemporary, George Thomason, buying them at a rate of two a day in 1641; in January 1642, he accumulated a massive 200 pamphlets in the space of just one month.[12]

While the explosion of printed material often represented the radical Puritan view, it also prompted a reaction from more moderate commentators who urged less extreme reform, resulting in what has been termed the 'paper war'.[13] Popular radicalism was, in effect, stimulating the growth of sympathy for the King and gained him support on the streets. However, in 1641 important elections in the City returned officials who supported Pym and so control of London, including command of the Trained Bands (London's militia), was now safely on the side of popular radicalism.

**Key term**

**enclosure:** the act of fencing in land that was previously used as common land. This process often caused tension between the local landowners and the common people.

# Conflicts between Crown and Parliament

As events developed throughout 1640–42 the King was by no means a passive observer but rather took actions that were clear attempts to impose his authority and regain the initiative.

## Attempts to impose royal authority and the development of a Royalist party

As the initial attacks on Laud and Wentworth erupted, Charles was willing to disarm his opponents by offering them key positions in government. The Earl of Bedford was the key architect of this plan. As Pym's patron he had suggested Pym be made Chancellor of the Exchequer and Oliver St John (who had defended Hampden in the Ship Money case) would be made Solicitor-General. However, on 9 May 1641 Bedford unexpectedly died of smallpox and with him died any chance of bringing Charles and his opponents together in such a way.

The most powerful means Charles had to assert his royal authority was to portray himself as the embodiment of law, order and religious moderation. Even those who had opposed the Personal Rule could, after the initial concessions of 1641, legitimately support the King against what increasingly appeared to be the radical and unlawful actions of 'King Pym', as his critics termed him.[14] As early as 25 January 1641, Charles, having made no attempt to prevent the imprisonment of Laud, promised to defend 'the true Protestant religion by law established without any connivance of popery or innovation … [and to] reduce all matters of religion and government to what they were in the purest times of Queen Elizabeth's days.'[15] With the Laudian bishops replaced, many moderate Anglicans who were eager to preserve the Church in its current form were now happy to support the King. As already noted, the division of MPs over the Root and Branch Petition neatly illustrates this shift in opinion. For many, the zealous innovations in religion advocated by Pym's allies were too much to be borne (see Voices from the past: Sir Thomas Aston). This support from moderates allowed the basis for a Royalist party to emerge, both in Parliament and the country at large. Votes on the Root and Branch Petition and the Grand Remonstrance saw two sides emerge and with it an important step towards civil war was taken.

## The execution of Strafford and its political consequences

On the evening of 12 May 1641, windows throughout the kingdom glowed as candles were lit to celebrate the execution of Thomas Wentworth, Earl of Strafford. As his head was lifted to the crowd it was met with cheers and many could have been forgiven for thinking that his execution would mark the beginning of a happy reconciliation between King and Parliament. Yet Wentworth's last words proved to be prophetic: 'I wish that every man would lay his hand on his heart and consider seriously whether the beginnings of the people's happiness should be written in letters of blood.' In time Wentworth's doubts proved to be right and his death did little to avert growing calamity[18]

---

### 💬 Voices from the past

#### *Sir Thomas Aston*

Aston's *Remonstrance against Presbytery* and the *Remonstrance and Petition of the County of Huntingdon* both show the suspicion many Anglicans had of Puritan 'innovation' and reform. In 1641 Aston wrote:

Under pretext of reforming the Church, the true aim of such spirits is to shake off the yoke of all obedience, either to ecclesiastical, civil, common, statute or customary laws of the kingdom and to introduce a mere arbitrary government.[16]

Charles sorely regretted having signed the death warrant of his most loyal servant yet had done so at the urging of his advisors and because the growing anger of the London mob outside the Palace of Whitehall threatened the safety of the royal family. Wentworth himself had written urging the King to sign. The decision haunted Charles to the last: when he too faced the executioner's axe in 1649, he was heard to say that 'an unjust sentence that I suffered to take effect is punished now by an unjust sentence on me'.[19] The great irony was, however, that Wentworth's execution actually served to sharpen the conflict. Up to this point the attack on the 'evil counsellors' had meant that MPs had been able to present a united force; yet, with Wentworth dead and Laud imprisoned, all future criticism was directed towards the King himself. This was too much for moderate MPs to stomach and they now moved increasingly to defend the King, and so made conflict possible.

## The slide into war

### The impact of events in Ireland

The outbreak of the Irish Rebellion in late October 1641 had consequences beyond its immediate violence. In addition to providing the backdrop to Pym's Grand Remonstrance, events in Ireland raised the need to provide funds for an army to suppress the rebellion. It divided Pym's junto and what would become a distinct Royalist party led by MPs like Edward Hyde. In the discussions that emerged around the Grand Remonstrance and the need for an army the fundamental question arose of who should control it. It was the opinion of Sir Arthur Hesilrige, one of Pym's allies, that any general appointed to command troops should be agreed by Parliament. This, however, ran counter to the law that normally allowed the monarch to appoint commanders as they saw fit. Neither side was willing to concede, and this led to the sharp division in Parliament in the vote on the Grand Remonstrance and the King's outright rejection of it in December 1641.

Another consequence of the Irish Rebellion was that it raised tensions in London. On 27 December the mob, agitated by Catholic atrocities in Ulster, prevented bishops from taking their seats in the House of Lords. The bishops petitioned the King to declare all business conducted in their absence null and void but were promptly impeached by Parliament for their efforts. Charles must have realised that things were getting out of control when rumours circulated that the Queen herself was to be impeached for being a key leader in a Catholic conspiracy. One last attempt was made by the King on 2 January 1642 to win Pym over by offering him the post of Chancellor of the Exchequer, but Pym refused. The next day, having been manouevred into an impossible situation, the King drew up charges of high treason against five leading MPs, Pym, Hesilrige, Holles, Hampden and Strode, as well as Lord Mandeville (later the Earl of Manchester), for having sought 'to subvert the fundamental laws and government of England'. When the men were not delivered into custody, the King decided to act.[20]

## ACTIVITY 3.8

Read the extracts in Voices from the past: Sir Thomas Aston and Voices from the past: The people of Huntingdon. Why do Sir Thomas Aston and the people of Huntingdon see Pym and his Puritan allies as dangerous?

### Voices from the past

#### The people of Huntingdon

*The Petition of the County of Huntingdon*

Similarly, in 1642, the people of Huntingdon responded to many petitions that had called for the abolition of bishops by declaring that such an action was a:

subversion of that order and form of divine service which hath happily continued amongst us ever since the reformation of religion. Out of a tender and zealous regard hereunto, we have thought it our duty not only to disavow all such petitions, but also to manifest our public affections, and desires to continue ... the present government of the Church.[17]

## The failed arrest of the Five Members

On the afternoon of 4 January 1642, King Charles marched on Parliament accompanied by an armed bodyguard, probably 200 or 300 strong. Charles believed that if the ringleaders of the parliamentary opposition could be removed, all his troubles would be over. This was a high-risk move and was dependent on success. In a moment of great tension, Charles entered the chamber of the House of Commons. Despite politely uncovering his head and bowing to either side, there was no covering up the fact that this was a flagrant breach of parliamentary privilege. Not only was Charles interrupting the Commons' debate but he also sought to ignore MPs' immunity to arrest while Parliament was sitting. When he queried the whereabouts of the accused members, the King was respectfully told by Speaker Lenthall that he could only see and speak as the House instructed him; the King famously responded that his eyes were as good as any other and that he could see the 'birds had flown'.[21] In fact the MPs, having been tipped off, had only narrowly avoided arrest by escaping from Westminster by river.

The next day the King entered the City of London and at the Guildhall demanded that the city officials hand over the accused MPs for arrest. Cries of 'God save the King!' were soon drowned out by cries of 'Privileges of Parliament!' The King, acutely aware that he had lost control of the capital, grew fearful for the safety of his family and left London. His abandonment of the capital stimulated a physical divide that ensured that 'civil war seemed likely if not inevitable'.[22]

## Local grievances

John Morrill's study of the impact of war on the provinces has highlighted that the main reaction to the growing crisis in London was shock at what seemed to be 'the collapse of order'.[23] In the provinces enclosure riots peaked, sometimes because old grievances were given the chance to be played out, and sometimes because the targets of people's anger were bound up in the very nature of the conflict. The Countess of Rivers, for example, was targeted for being a Catholic. As each side began to pursue a 'paper war' of pamphlets and petitions against the other, local pamphlets and newssheets echoed the language of the London press and political leaders; depending on their outlook they spoke popish plots or Puritanical zeal that risked the future of the English Church.

Some counties showed their dissatisfaction with the conflict itself. The gentry of Devon declared that the claims of both sides to defend the true religion and safeguard the constitution were so similar that they could not choose between them. So wedded to peace was the attitude of so many people that neutrality, or a refusal to declare for one side or another, became commonplace. Michael Braddick has pointed out that the conflict was essentially a mutual war of defence, with both sides fighting to prevent the calamity they thought the other side would bring. The same was true for the moderate majority and in the first eight months of 1642 all but two English counties petitioned for peace. The general desire for peace, however, was drowned out as attempts at negotiation failed and the drums of war grew louder.

## Failure of negotiations between the King and the Long Parliament

As tensions grew, attempted reconciliation became less likely, largely because both sides were driven by their own conspiracy theories. The 'Puritan-Parliamentarian' theory argued that the King's followers were driven by a Catholic plot to reverse the English Reformation and establish an absolute monarchy. Against them was the 'Anglican-Royalist' argument that the Anglican Church was at risk from Puritan 'schismatics' (people willing to break up the unity of English Protestants) and fundamentally alter the constitutional balance of the King, Lords and Commons. The trouble was that both sides vehemently believed their own propaganda and so every move the opposition made to get the upper hand only seemed to prove their fears.

This mutual fear explains why Parliament's initial offer of peace, *the Nineteen Propositions* offered to Charles on 2 June, was so hardline in demanding parliamentary control of key appointments and the army. But the same can be said of Charles's rejection of the offer. In publishing his *Answer to the XIX Propositions*, Charles argued that the *Propositions* sought the disruption of the 'ancient, equal, happy, well-poised … constitution of the government of this kingdom'.[24] In rejecting Parliament's offer, the King gave voice to the motives of many who rallied to his banner, and who have been termed 'constitutional royalists'.

In creating monsters of their enemies both sides ensured that any opportunity for a negotiated peace was limited. This was made still worse by the seemingly aggressive moves of both sides in raising forces and by the Queen's selling of royal jewels in Amsterdam to raise funds for war. Above all, a negotiated peace failed because both sides believed that they could win. Both sides dreamt of a single sharp victory to resolve the matter and so neither was willing to compromise.

## Military preparations for war

With the King gone, Parliamentarian MPs and Lords assumed the right to pass laws through the passage of **ordinances**. One of the most important was the Militia Ordinance of 5 March 1642. Claiming the King was 'seduced by evil counsel' it placed all military forces under Parliamentary control and when put into operation two months later it gave Parliament's lieutenants the right to raise troops. This provocation resulted in the King's own preparations to raise troops by issuing Commissions of Array in June. These commissions entitled members of the gentry and the nobility to raise troops in the King's name.

By abandoning London the King had effectively given Parliament a head start in the preparations for war. The Parliamentarians controlled not only the **London Trained Bands** that guarded the capital but also the Tower of London, with its magazine of gunpowder and arsenal of weapons. The King, having made slow progress northwards, finally decided to seize the arsenal at Hull, only to be refused entry by Sir John Hotham. The growing seriousness of the situation finally persuaded Parliament that it should raise an army of 10 000 volunteers and three days later, on 12 July, it appointed the Earl of Essex as Lord General. The next month, in a medieval act of pageantry and theatre, the King raised his royal standard at Nottingham and began to gather forces around him. The stage was finally set for war. Bulstrode Whitelock, startled by the speed with which events had unfolded, wrote in disbelief about the state England now found itself in.

---

**ACTIVITY 3.9**

Read Bulstrode Whitelock in Voices from the past and then consider the following questions.

1. What do you think were the 'unexpected accidents' and 'paper combats' that Whitelock refers to?

2. What does this account reveal about popular attitudes to the conflict?

3. Why is this a particularly useful source for telling us about popular reluctance to enter war?

---

**Key term**

**London Trained Bands:** companies of London Militia that had existed before the civil war. They were made up of citizens of the capital who could be called to arms in moments of crisis. They held a regular calendar of drills and training, hence the name. They were controlled by the City of London and were not part of the New Model Army.

---

**Voices from the past**

### *Bulstrode Whitelock MP*

Bulstrode Whitelock MP was a keen opponent of the Personal Rule. He had drawn up the charges for the impeachment of Wentworth and had voted in support of the Grand Remonstrance.

We have slid into the beginnings of a civil war by one unexpected accident after another so that we scarcely know how we have come this far; but from paper combats … We are now come to the question of raising forces.[25]

## Further reading

An excellent summary of the key events can be found in Smith DL. *A History of the Modern British Isles, 1603–1707.* Oxford: Blackwell; 1998. As in Chapter 2, a more detailed narrative can be found in Braddick M. *God's Fury, England's Fire: A New History of the English Civil Wars.* London: Penguin; 2009. The view of events told through the experiences of contemporaries is evocatively conjured up in Purkiss D. *The English Civil War: A People's History.* London: Harper Perennial; 2007. Lindley K. *The English Civil War and Revolution: A Sourcebook.* London: Routledge; 1998 contains a useful selection of primary sources.

### Practice essay questions

1. 'The Grand Remonstrance was the turning point in the decline into war by 1642.' Explain why you agree or disagree with this view.
2. 'Parliament was to blame for the breakdown in relations between Crown and Parliament, 1640–42.' Explain why you agree or disagree with this view.
3. 'Charles's unwillingness to make concessions was the reason for deteriorating relations with Parliament, 1640–42.' Assess the validity of this view.
4. With reference to these extracts and your understanding of the historical context, which of these two sources is more valuable for explaining Parliamentary opposition to the King in the period 1640–42?

## Extract A

Richard Baxter, a puritan minister, recorded his impression of the Short Parliament in 1640.[26]

They made long and vehement speeches against the ship money and against the Judges that gave their judgement for it, and against the Et Cetera oath and the bishops and convocation that were the formers of it; but especially against the Lord Thomas Wentworth, Lord Deputy of Ireland and Dr. Laud, Archbishop of Canterbury, as evil councillors, the cause of all.

## Extract B

John Pym's speech to the House of Commons, 7 November 1640.[27]

[There is] a design to alter the kingdom both in religion and government. This is the highest of treason, this blows up by piecemeal, and almost goeth through [to] their ends. This concerns the king as well as we, and that I say with reverence and care of his Majesty.

## Chapter summary

By the end of this chapter you should have gained an understanding of how Charles and his Parliament slipped from political crisis into a state of war. In particular you should be able to:

- describe the role played by the King and parliamentary opposition
- identify the points at which parliamentary unity collapsed and the creation of two sides became a reality
- explain the King's failure to keep in control of his capital city
- give evidence of how both sides contributed to growing tensions.

## End notes

1  Quoted in Braddick M. *God's Fury, England's Fire: A New History of the English Civil Wars*. London: Penguin Books; 2009. p. 115

2  Sylvester M. *Reliquiae Baxterianae*, 'The Life of the Reverend Mr Richard Baxter'. Lib. I, Part I. London; 1696. p. 18.

3  Ibid.

4  Purkiss D. *The English Civil War*. London: Harper Perennial; 2007. p. 117.

5  Miller J. *The English Civil Wars: Roundheads, Cavaliers and the Execution of the King*. London: Robinson; 2009. p. 58.

6  Lord Digby quoted in Smith DL. *A History of the Modern British Isles, 1603–1707*. Oxford: Blackwell; 1998. p. 116.

7  Braddick M. *God's Fury, England's Fire*. p. 174. Also at https://mercuriuspoliticus.files.wordpress.com/2008/01/treason.jpg.

8  Ibid. p. 170–71.

9  Quoted in Smith DL. *A History of the Modern British Isles, 1603–1707*. p. 123.

10  Purkiss D. *The English Civil War*. p. 121.

11  Hibbert C. *Charles I: A Life of Religion, War and Treason*. London: Palgrave Macmillan; 2007. p. 155.

12  Braddick M. *God's Fury, England's Fire*. p. 172–73.

13  Ibid. p. 173.

14  Smith DL. *Constitutional Royalism and the Search for Settlement, c. 1640–1649*. Cambridge: CUP; 2002. p. 62–63.

15  Smith DL. *A History of the Modern British Isles, 1603–1707*. Oxford: OUP; 1998. p. 119.

16  Quoted in Lindley K. *The English Civil War and Revolution: A Sourcebook*. London: Routledge; 1998. p. 62–63.

17  Ibid.

18  Purkiss D. *The English Civil War. p. 117*.

19  Quoted in Hibbert C. *Charles I*. p. 155–57.

20  Quoted in Smith DL. *A History of the Modern British Isles*, 1603–1707. p. 124.

21  Quoted in Lindley K. *The English Civil War and Revolution*. p. 76–77.

22  Quoted in Worden B. *The English Civil Wars, 1640–1660*. p. 40.

23  Morrill J. *Revolt in the Provinces: The People of England and the Tragedies of War, 1630–1648*. 2nd edition. London: Longman; 1999. p. 184.

24  Quoted in Smith DL. *A History of the Modern British Isles, 1603–1707*. p. 83.

25  Whitelocke B. *Memorials of the English Affairs*. London; 1682. p. 58.

26  Sylvester M. *Reliquiae Baxterianae*, 'The Life of the Reverend Mr Richard Baxter'. Lib. I, Part I, 1696. p. 18.

27  Kenyon JP. *The Stuart Constitution, 1603–1688: Documents and Commentary*. Cambridge: CUP; 1986. p. 189.

# 4 War and radicalism, 1642–1646

In this section we will examine the progress of the First Civil War and rise of radicalism. We will look into:

- The First Civil War: the strengths and weaknesses of the political and military leadership of the Royalist cause.
- The First Civil War: the strengths and weaknesses of the political and military leadership of the Parliamentary forces; emergence of the New Model Army; the Solemn League and Covenant; the Self-denying Ordinance.
- The intensification of radicalism: popular radicalism in London; religious radicalism in the New Model Army; pamphlets and propaganda.
- The end of the First Civil War: divisions among the Parliamentary leaders; attempts at settlement; the capture of Charles I.

## Introduction

Few people in England had foreseen that the clash between the King and his Parliament would end in civil war. Nevertheless, as the winter of 1642 turned to spring, the land awoke to the sounds of martial music and marching feet as both sides raised troops in defence of their cause. In this chapter we will explore the military innovations of Parliament and the growing divisions in leadership that would have a major influence in the post-war period. Against the backdrop of war, radical religious and social ideas emerged and we will examine how these ideas began to circulate in society and Parliament's New Model Army.

## Timeline

| 1642 | **23 October:** indecisive Battle of Edgehill <br> **13 November:** Charles's advance towards London halted at Turnham |
|------|------|
| 1643 | **1 February–14 April:** Treaty of Oxford; unsuccessful peace talks <br> **24 February:** Parliament introduces weekly (later monthly) assessment <br> **15 September:** Ormond concludes 'cessation' with the Irish on Charles's behalf <br> **25 September:** Solemn League and Covenant <br> **8 December:** death of John Pym |
| 1644 | **19 January:** Earl of Leven leads Scottish covenanter army of 21 000 troops into England <br> **16 February:** Committee of Both Kingdoms established <br> **2 July:** Parliamentarian/Scottish victory at Marston Moor near York; Royalists lose control of the north <br> **27 October:** indecisive second Battle of Newbury <br> **November–December:** major public quarrel between Cromwell and Manchester over conduct of war; 'Self-denying Ordinance' proposed |
| 1645 | **30 January–22 February:** Treaty of Uxbridge; unsuccessful peace talks <br> **17 February:** New Model Army created <br> **3 April:** Self-Denying Ordinance; Cromwell subsequently receives a series of short-term exemptions <br> **14 June:** New Model Army defeats Royalist forces at Naseby <br> **25 August:** King concludes second 'cessation' with the Irish Confederates; concessions promised to Catholics in return for troops to assist Charles on the mainland |
| 1646 | **5 May:** Charles surrenders to Scots at Newark <br> **24 June:** Oxford surrenders; end of First Civil War |

# The First Civil War

## The strengths and weaknesses of the political and military leadership of the Royalist cause

Some suggest the first victim of war may have been a weaver from Manchester, killed in July 1642 while repulsing royalist attempts to take the town. Others have noted the case of a Northamptonshire farmer who, when asked which side he favoured, had replied that he was for the king *and* Parliament. Dissatisfied by his answer the royalist troopers shot him. Either way, the spilling of blood in local disputes during the raising of troops in the summer of 1642 marked the beginning of what would become known as the First Civil War (1642–46). The bloodshed was unprecedented and proportionately it inflicted greater losses on the population than the First World War nearly 300 years later. From a British rather than an English perspective, blood had already been spilled in the Bishops' Wars and the Irish Rebellion, but it was the conflict that began in England in 1642 that proved decisive.

### The nature of civil war armies
The war was fought by armies typical of the period and made up of **cavalry, artillery** and **infantry**. The cavalry were the armies' shock-weapon. The theory was that they would defeat the enemy's cavalry on its flanks before turning in to crush the infantry and artillery at the centre. Artillery was notoriously inaccurate and slow to reload but was invaluable when laying siege to fortifications; major field armies were considered

incomplete without at least a few cannons. Most important, however, was the infantry, or foot soldiers, who were most numerous, least well-provisioned and trained, and whose pikemen and musketeers bore the brunt of the fighting. The armies were divided into regiments commanded by a colonel, numbering anything up to 1000 men. Until the formation of the New Model Army in 1645 both Royalist and Parliamentarian armies looked almost identical, dressed as they were in a mixture of military and civilian clothing. Figure 4.1 shows the battle of Naseby, with armies drawn up with infantry regiments and artillery in the centre and troops of cavalry on the flanks, the standard deployment used by both armies.

## Royalist advantages

By the late summer of 1642 the King's force was comparable in size to the Parliamentarian army raised by the Earl of Essex and enjoyed some considerable early advantages. Most notable were the experienced officers from the Thirty Years' War. Many of these arrived with the King's formidable young nephew, Prince Rupert, Count Palatine of the Rhine. Having fought in the wars of religion these men were well trained and shaped the King's volunteers (and later conscripts) into an effective fighting force. Rupert also brought hundreds of cavalry horses to supplement the many mounts provided by royalist gentry and nobility. Horses suitable for cavalry were expensive and while stock lasted were an important advantage enjoyed by royalist regiments of horse.

One important advantage that the royalist forces enjoyed was a clear focus for their strategy – to take London. In Autumn 1642 the King seized the initiative by advancing on London and placing himself between the Earl of Essex and the capital. On 23 October the two armies clashed at the battle of Edgehill. After the royalist

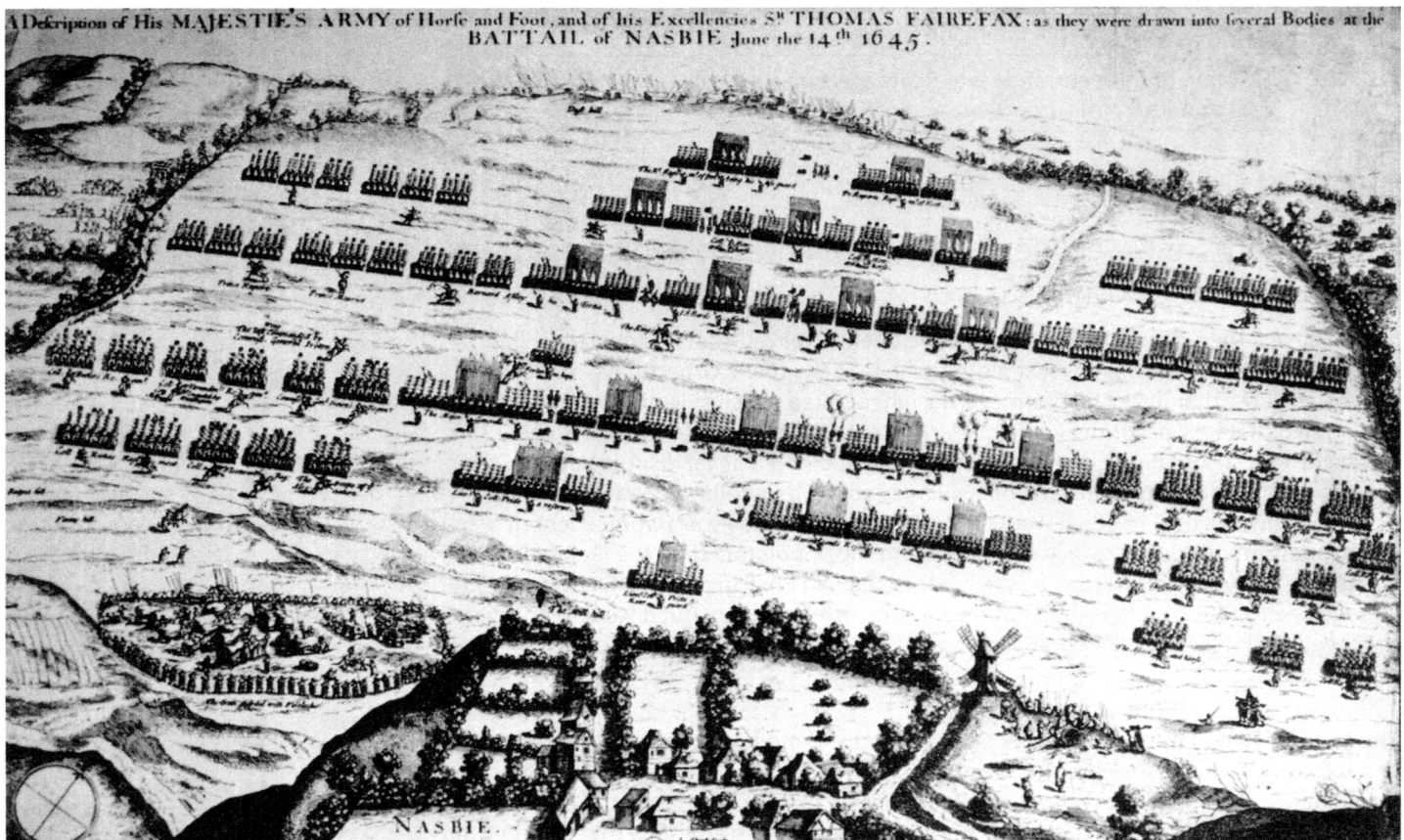

**Figure 4.1:** Civil war soldiers drawn up for battle. A stylised depiction of Naseby, 1645.

cavalry swept the opposing cavalry from the field, Prince Rupert failed to rally them. Instead, they pursued the fleeing Parliamentarian troopers miles to the rear where they proceeded to plunder the army's baggage train. In their absence, the infantry fought each other to a bloody standstill and under the cover of darkness the Earl of Essex eventually withdrew his battered army. In the weeks that followed almost instant victory was snatched from the King's grasp when his slow advance on London was halted at Turnham Green – Parliament having had time to prepare a defensive. The King turned back and established his capital at Oxford.

As 1643 progressed, the central strategy of capturing London provided a focus for the three main royalist armies – the King's army at Oxford, Sir Ralph Hopton's army in the southwest, and the Marquess of Newcastle's army in the north. This coordinated, three-pronged advance on the capital at first proved highly successful: in the north Newcastle scored a victory at Adwalton Moor (30 June) bringing Yorkshire under royalist control; in the southwest Hopton crushed Waller's Parliamentarians at the battles of Landsdown (5 July) and Roundway Down (13 July); and most importantly on 26 July Rupert successfully took Bristol, England's second most important port. North of the border the royalist war effort benefited from the Earl of Montrose's campaigns in Scotland, which remained a thorn in the side of those Covenanters like Argyll and Leven who were to support Parliament later in the war.

The early royalist war effort was also bolstered by a combined political and military command structure. The King and his central administration at Oxford ensured that in the first two years there was a certain degree of clarity in royalist planning and the King was able to assert authority over his followers. This was seen in 1644 when the King, eager to appear moderate, called an alternative Parliament to assemble in Oxford. When it urged a policy of negotiated peace, the King was able to assert his will and push on with a strategy based on military victory.

The central administration was supported by local committees, which used pre-war taxation methods and structures to raise revenue. The King's treasury was further enhanced by a series of valuable donations made by wealthy supporters such as the Earl of Worcester who gave the King a massive £900 000 (the equivalent of four or five parliamentary subsidies).

The King also drew support from Ireland in the form of the Protestant troops commanded by the Earl of Ormond, the royal ward in Ireland. In reality, Ormond was able to give only limited assistance, and what troops he could send often had to be transported piecemeal in order to prevent intervention by the navy, which had declared for Parliament. Thus, no single army from Ireland ever materialised on the British mainland. What did materialise, however, was the bad press that greeted Charles's attempt to use Irish troops. Although Ormond's troops were Protestant, they were only available because Charles was willing to reach a truce with the Catholic rebels and this reflected badly on the King. In 1645 Charles even entered negotiations with the Catholic rebels in the hope that they would provide military assistance. Although this came to nothing, the damage it did to the King was enormous.

**Figure 4.2:** Charles I is depicted holding a council of war. The commander seated at the table is Prince Rupert, the King's nephew. Although only 23 at the start of the war, Rupert was a talented military commander. He was demonised by Parliamentarian propagandists who claimed that his pet dog was the devil incarnate.

## Discussion point

In this imagined scene, how does the artist try to portray the royalist advantages enjoyed in the early years of the war?

### Royalist weaknesses

It is clear that the King enjoyed the military and strategic advantage in the first two years of the war; however, the longer the war dragged, on the more apparent royalist weaknesses became. By the end of 1643 the King's central strategy of taking the capital began to collapse. Royalist commanders became increasingly distracted by defeating Parliamentary forces in the provinces and so their efforts became divided. This was coupled with growing discord among royalist leaders. On the one hand there were moderates, like Edward Hyde, who urged the King to push for a negotiated peace. Against them were hardliners like Lord Digby and Prince Rupert, who urged the King to seek total military victory. The latter were supported by the Queen, who urged the King to defeat the 'traitors' utterly. Furthermore, the hardliners were themselves far from united, due to character clashes between Digby and Rupert.

Royalist financial difficulties grew as the war progressed. Loans began to dry up as the loyal supporters who had given so generously were no longer at home managing their estates. Regular taxation of royalist zones of control provided the main income but this was significantly less than that raised by Parliament; the King's territories in the north and west tended to be less wealthy than the southern and eastern counties controlled by Parliament. The King was lenient in extracting funds and the nature of the royalist tax system meant that the cost of local defence and administration was deducted from the revenue sent to the King's central treasury in Oxford. Moreover, widespread plundering of civilians by both sides in the civil war hampered the ability of many civilians to pay the taxes demanded. These financial pressures made it hard for Charles to purchase or produce the goods required to fight the war, and poor and irregular pay led to desertion and forced impressment of men who had no wish to volunteer.

## The strengths and weaknesses of the political and military leadership of the Parliamentary forces

### Parliamentary weaknesses

While the King was in a strong position at the start of the conflict, the opposite was true of Parliament's forces. From the outset Parliament had to work hard to legitimise its military resistance to the King and all too often appeared as rebels and traitors. Just as non-parliamentary taxation had been illegal, so too was raising forces against a rightful king.

The most pressing weakness was the division of Parliamentarian armies into local association armies, tied to the regions that supported them. Alongside the Earl of Essex's army operating in the Midlands and defending London, there was also the Western Association army, the Northern Association army and the Eastern Association, commanded by the Earl of Manchester. It was in the latter that Oliver Cromwell enjoyed great success as a cavalry commander. These armies operated independently and the central parliamentary committee that tried to manage the war was a poor substitute for an overall commander-in-chief. The most crippling weakness, however, was that many of the officers were in fact politicians, sitting either as MPs or Lords. Although many of the commanders were brave, and at times skilful, politicians were not always the most gifted soldiers.

In Parliament, MPs in Westminster were hardly any better. They soon descended into factional in-fighting and directionless committees. What Parliament clearly lacked was a clear objective; was it aiming for total military victory over the royalists or was it simply putting up a show of military resistance in order to aid the peace negotiations that would follow? Some found comfort in the idea that they were fighting to free the King from the clutches of his 'evil advisors', while others felt they were fighting to safeguard either the English Reformation or the political stability of the ancient constitution. Although republicans were few in number, the occasional extremist, like the republican Henry Marten, served to divide MPs, many of whom were frightened of total victory in case it brought wholesale change to the constitution and monarchy. In short, nobody knew what victory would look like. Above all, after 1643, once Pym was dead of cancer and with Hampden killed in battle, Parliament lacked a leader to bind them together (see the section on Divisions among the parliamentary leaders).

### Parliamentarian strengths

Despite such disorder, by 1643 some sense of direction was being found. Before Pym died he was instrumental in establishing regular taxes through weekly and monthly **assessments** that were ruthlessly collected by new county committees. Efficiency also improved. In 1644 a Committee of Both Kingdoms was established to conduct a joint war effort. At the same time Parliamentarian control of the navy began to be felt.

Control of the navy and domination of the coast hampered royalist supplies. Meanwhile London, with its arsenal at the Tower, continued to provide Parliament with the means to produce black powder and weapons. In addition, City traders provided considerable income in the form of loans and taxes and so the longer the war proceeded, the more financially effective Parliament's war effort became. The victory at Marston Moor on 2 July 1644 saw Parliamentarians gain control of the north. This proved what could be achieved if local Association armies combined under professional and talented commanders like Fairfax and Cromwell. It was Parliament's failure to grasp the military advantage after this battle that drove men like Cromwell to take action and bring about real military reforms that would ensure victory in the future.

---

**ACTIVITY 4.1**

1. Using the information presented in the section on the strengths and weaknesses of the political and military leadership of the Royalist cause, draw up lists of the strengths and weaknesses.

2. Why were Royalists better suited to a short war?

---

🔑 **Key term**

**assessments:** the term used to describe a parliamentary tax. Counties were 'assessed' for how much tax they owed. It was then up to the local officials to assess how much individuals in their region were eligible to pay. Parliamentary taxes tended to be judged on a weekly or monthly basis.

One final phenomenon that served to strengthen Parliament's efforts was the growth of neutralism. As the war dragged on, more people turned to neutralism. Many counties signed non-aggression pacts and from 1644 some began to raise **'Clubmen'** to defend against both sides thus restricting the areas from which taxes could be raised. This was a great benefit to Parliament whose greater financial resources meant it could weather the storm more easily than the Royalists who, by the latter half of the war, were beginning to lack the funds to continue.

## Key term

**Clubmen:** first formed in 1644, these associations were local forces raised by communities to keep out the armies of both sides. They were the ultimate expression of neutralism.

## ACTIVITY 4.2

1. Using the information presented in the section on The strengths and weaknesses of the political and military leadership of the Parliamentary forces, draw up lists of Parliamentarian strengths and weaknesses.

2. Why were Parliamentarians better suited to a long war?

**Figure 4.3:** Cromwell and his 'Ironsides' at Marston Moor, 1644. The victory at Marston Moor helped bring about the Royalist surrender of York and proved the worth of commanders like Cromwell, who led his cavalry with distinction in the battle.

## Emergence of the New Model Army

In 1645 the Committee of Both Kingdoms, which commanded the Parliamentarian war effort, decided on a major overhaul of three of its southern and eastern Association armies. Neither the Earl of Essex's army nor those of the Earl of Manchester and Sir William Waller had proved effective. The committee decided to remodel the armies as one force under the command of the talented and respected Sir Thomas Fairfax, who was appointed Lord General.

The key distinction was that its officers were appointed based on ability, and its soldiers experienced stricter military discipline in exchange for regular pay. All infantry regiments were also to be given red uniforms for which the British Army became famous in the centuries to come. The New Model Army acquired a reputation for radical religious beliefs; spurred on by their battlefield successes they believed they were the embodiment of God's will. However, as John Morrill has suggested, 'professionalisation, not radicalisation, was the key'.

## The Solemn League and Covenant

Negotiations between Pym and leading Scottish Covenanters led to Parliament signing the Solemn League and Covenant in September 1643 and resulted in an army of 21 000 men under the Earl of Leven crossing the border in January 1644. They added their force to the campaign against northern Royalists and ultimately contributed to the great victory at Marston Moor.

For the Scots, the Solemn League and Covenant was primarily an agreement that pledged to 'bring the Churches of God in the three kingdoms to the nearest conjunction and uniformity in religion'.[1] As such it ensured that the Churches of England and Ireland would be reformed along Presbyterian lines. To the English, the alliance was more important in terms of the troops that it would bring to help reverse the Parliamentarian losses of 1643. English fears of Scottish Presbyterians were finally overcome when Henry Vane, a Parliamentary negotiator, changed the wording of the promise to reform the English Church, using the phrase, 'according to the word of God'.[2] The Scots assumed wrongly that this would result in England adopting Presbyterianism, whereas to the reluctant English MPs it meant that there would be plenty of space to wriggle out of the agreement at a later date. In the interim, Parliament established the Westminster Assembly, made up of 125 church ministers and eight Scottish observers, to discuss religious reforms. In time, the Scots, who had hoped that the Solemn League and Covenant would act as 'God's dishcloth' to cleanse the land of all forms of popery, became disappointed by the half-hearted English experiments with Presbyterianism.[3]

## The Self-denying Ordinance

Following the decision to create the New Model Army, the Self-denying Ordinance (April 1645) decreed that all military commanders who were also MPs or Lords should give up their ranks as officers. As we will see in the section on Divisions between the Parliamentary leaders later in this chapter, tension between Parliamentarian leaders had grown serious over the mishandling of a number of military campaigns by the Earls of Essex and Manchester. Criticism of their leadership was sharp; Cromwell, among others, voiced his opposition to such men retaining their commands.

The Ordinance began the transformation of the army into an increasingly **meritocratic** force in which officers of known ability, as well as sound Protestant views, would receive promotion. Philip Skippon is a good example; having served in the Thirty Years' War, he was appointed Sergeant-Major General of Infantry. In a twist of irony, however, the Ordinance also denied rank to Cromwell and his son-in-law, Henry Ireton, two MPs who had served with distinction. The Ordinance would certainly have robbed the New Model Army of its best cavalry commander had Parliament (at the urging of Fairfax) not given a series of exemptions for these two men, thus allowing them to continue as both soldiers and politicians.

Cromwell's exemption and appointment as Lieutenant-General of Horse came just in time and by 14 June 1645 he was with Fairfax and the New Model Army at the climactic battle of Naseby. The battle saw the King's main field army confront the New Model Army for the first time. Although outnumbered, the King's veteran troops came close to breaking Fairfax's new force. Parliament's left flank was swept away by an impetuous charge by Prince Rupert's cavalry, whereas in the centre, Skippon's New Model infantry regiments began to break under the assault of Royalist infantry. Only on the right flank did Cromwell's cavalry defeat the opposing Royalist force. Unlike Rupert's cavalry, who once again lost control and chased the fleeing enemy from the field as they had done at Edgehill in 1642, Cromwell's disciplined troops wheeled around and struck the King's infantry on the flank and rear. Cromwell's action won the day and the King's infantry fought a desperate and bloody retreat. Charles, having tried personally to lead a last-ditch charge, eventually fled with his troops, leaving the wagons containing his personal correspondence to fall into Parliament's hands. It was the beginning of the end for the King.

## ACTIVITY 4.3

1. Using the information in the previous three sections, list the key changes brought about by Parliament to help win the war.

2. Look at your list. Are any of the changes connected? How?

3. Would Parliamentary victory have been likely without any one of the changes?

## Key term

**meritocratic:** this term describes a system that rewards the skills and achievements of an individual. The New Model Army was meritocratic because it appointed its officers on the basis of their abilities.

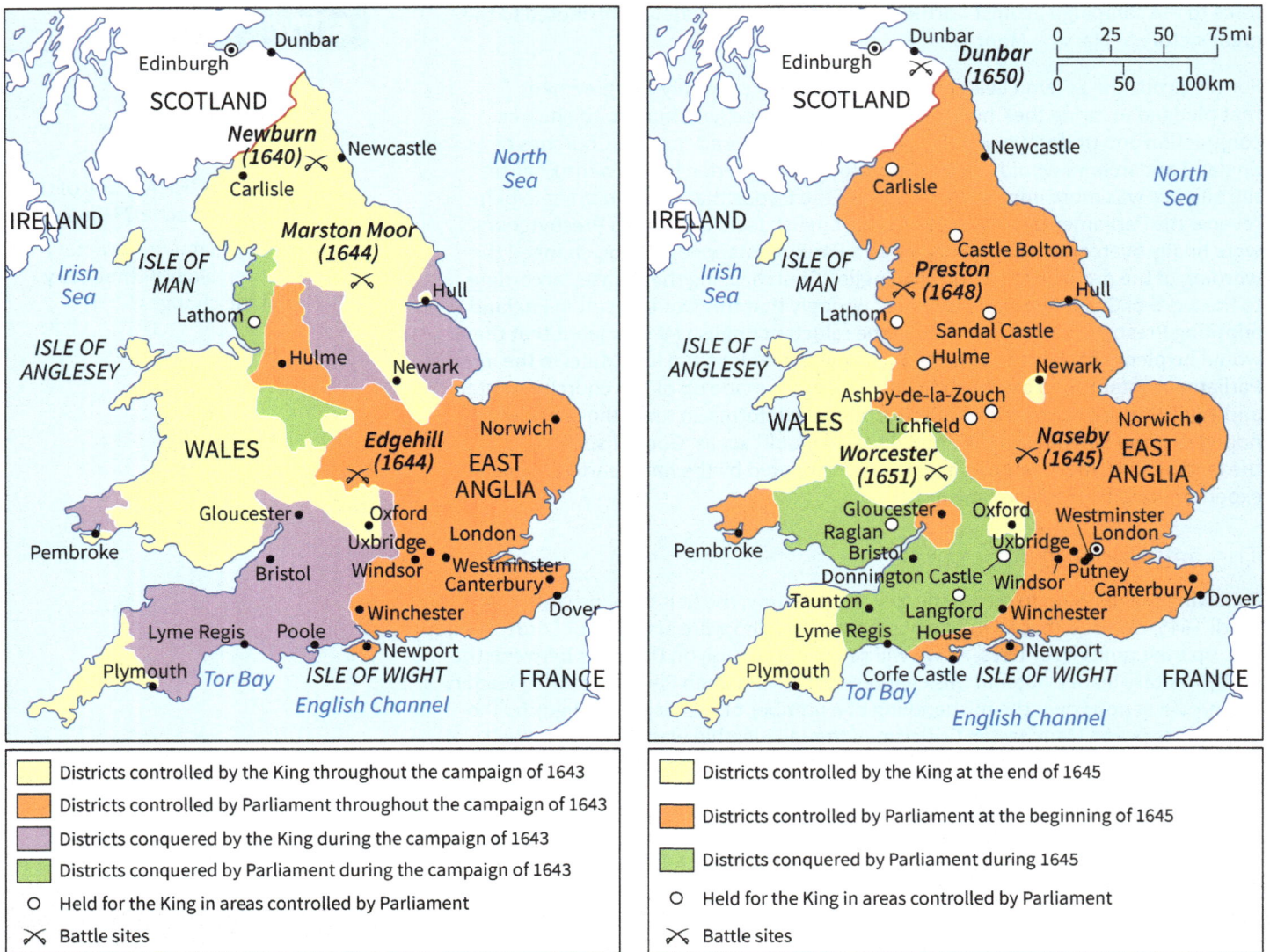

**Figure 4.4:** Strategic maps of the First Civil War in England. These two maps highlight the high point of the Royalist war effort in 1643, in contrast to the loss of control by the end of 1645.

## The intensification of radicalism

The horrors of war changed the way people looked at the world around them. Plundering, taxes and death left them yearning for the normality of the pre-war world. They wanted the King on his throne, respectful of his Parliament's wishes; 'they wanted the social order firm, the Church properly good and godly'; in short they felt the world had been 'turned upside down' and they wanted it put right again.[4] But for others, the chaos of war drove them to reimagine the world and Church. This reimagining was radicalism, and it found its home in London.

### Popular radicalism in London

From 1642 onwards London became fertile ground for radical ideas. Unlike rural areas, social hierarchy was less clear in London and this was diluted further by the influx of refugees seeking safety behind London's defences. The confusion of war set people's imagination alight, and this was fuelled by the constant belief that London was under threat: Londoners flocked to the Guildhall in their thousands to donate their savings and valuables while others toiled to help dig the giant earthwork fortifications that sprang up around the capital. Although London was never attacked, its population convinced itself that it was at the heart of events, and it was in this atmosphere that radical views exploded, led by the voices of men who became termed 'Levellers'. In 1645 and 1646 John Lilburne, Richard Overton and William Walwyn all published pamphlets that expressed their dissatisfaction with Parliament's efforts to reform the Church. Before long, the angry protests of the Levellers took on a socially radical tone, attacking what they saw to be a broken society in which no respect was given to the poor and lowly. In their eyes, the tyranny of the King had been replaced by the tyranny of a Parliament that trampled on the religious, political and legal freedoms of the English people.

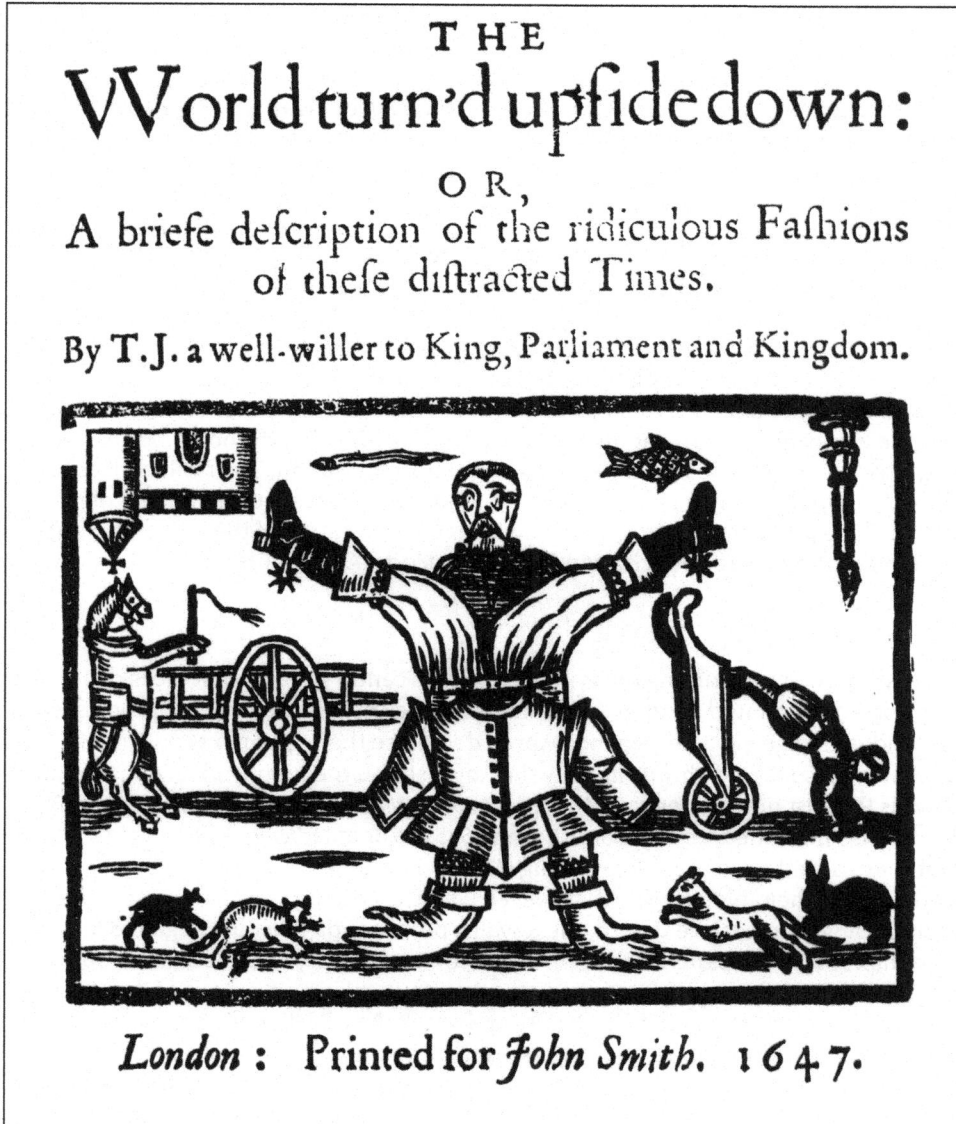

## THE
## World turn'd upfide down:
### OR,
A briefe defcription of the ridiculous Fafhions of thefe diftracted Times.

By **T.J.** a well-willer to King, Parliament and Kingdom.

London : Printed for *John Smith*. 1 6 4 7.

**Figure 4.5:** 'The World turned upside down', 1647. This popular print reveals the frustration felt by much of the population. War had turned society, Church and hierarchy on their head.

Radicalism also stimulated a conservative reaction. Many conservative Londoners believed the radicals only deepened society's wounds. This conservative feeling was seen in the peace protests led by London women who hoped for renewed prosperity

**ACTIVITY 4.4**

What did the soldiers do that shows they were aware of the religious aspects of the Civil War? Who were their actions aimed against?

**Key term**

**zeal:** used to describe the actions of someone who fervently believes in a cause, often at the expense of other interests. Someone who acted zealously (or with zeal) would be called a zealot.

**sectaries:** the term given to members of religious sects (see Table 5.1)

and trade. However, another important impact of London's radicalism was that it spread to the army's ranks.

## Religious radicalism in the New Model Army

It is not surprising that radicalism thrived in the highly religious New Model Army. Its soldiers saw the war as God's work, safeguarding the English Protestant Church from Catholicism. Even in the earliest days of the war soldiers had made their religious views clear, as the flags they carried showed religious images and mottos. For example, Captain Langrish's flag carried the motto 'I would die rather than be a papist'.[5] They also regularly committed iconoclasm in churches across the country (see Hidden voices: Nehemiah Wharton).

Radical religious beliefs in the army were reinforced by fasting, psalm-singing, prayer meetings, Bible study and preachers, all of which increased the religious **zeal** of the soldiers. This was helped by people's belief in **Providence** (the idea that God's will was acted out in people's actions on Earth). The New Model Army's victories in 1645 and 1646 convinced soldiers that they were God's instrument on Earth; increasingly, soldiers saw a parallel between themselves and the ancient Israelites of the Old Testament – God's chosen people.

Following the victory at Naseby, the radical voices grew so loud that one horrified Puritan minister, Richard Baxter, himself full of religious zeal, commented that things were spinning out of control (see Voices from the past: Richard Baxter). New groups, known as **sectaries**, were springing up including the Levellers, who favoured a levelling of society with equal distribution of wealth and no monarchy; Fifth Monarchists, who believed that Christ's return to Earth was imminent and He would rule the world; and Congregationalists, who believed the Church should be governed by individual congregations without any national organisation. Their willingness to voice their opinions grew stronger because many soldiers were owed arrears of pay, and so felt justified in asserting their views (for an exploration of the different groups see the section on The politicisation of the New Model Army in Chapter 5).

## Pamphlets and propaganda

The invention of the printing press in the previous century meant that ideas could now spread via printed cartoons, pamphlets and newssheets. As the war progressed both sides engaged in a propaganda war to demonise their opponents and justify their own reasons for fighting. Initially the Royalists led the propaganda war; the most famous Royalist newspaper was *Mercurius Aulicus*. Masterminded by John Birkenhead, *Aulicus* was published weekly from 1643 to 1645. So detailed were Birkenhead's stories that they caused major paranoia among MPs who became convinced that there were spies in their midst. By 1644, however, with the Earl of Essex's Parliamentarian army closing in to besiege Oxford, the Royalist propaganda machine began to falter. Pamphlets and newspapers slowed in production as military successes dried up. The rival Parliamentarian propagandists were not slow in taking advantage of the shifting tide of war and they went to great lengths to attack their rival publications. In May and June 1644 the Parliamentarian presses launched a scathing attack on the Royalist newspaper *Aulicus,* mocking it for its dwindling and desperate publications. The Parliamentary newspaper, *The Spie*, led the charge, claiming that, 'now since my Lord Generalls advance, the Pulse of *Aulicus* his braines beates very faintly and slowly; being hardly able to hold up his reputation with a single sheete'.[8] A few days later, *The Spie* announced that *Aulicus* had died, and *Mercurius Britannicus* triumphantly announced Parliamentary victory in the war of the newssheets (see Voices from the past: *Mercurius Britannicus*).

Parliament's great advantage came in 1645 when the King's private correspondence was captured at Naseby. Sensational publications of the King's letters in pamphlets

### Voices from the past

## *Mercurius Britannicus*

From a report in the Parliamentary newspaper, *Mercurius Britannicus*, 1644, claiming victory in the pamphlet war.

The advancement of his *Excellency* [the Earl of Essex], and Sir *William Waller* towards *Oxford* have broken the *braines* and the *heart* of their Intelligencer *Aulicus* … his pen dropt out of his hand, and himselfe dropt after it into his *Grave*; … thus *Britanicus* hath lived to see *Aulicus* die before him.[9]

titled *The King's Cabinet Opened* did much to rally support for Parliament's cause. The letters seemed to confirm people's worst fears: that the King was willing to make a deal with Irish Catholics and European powers against his own people.

So prolific were the propaganda pamphlets and newspapers that one contemporary managed to collect 4044 newssheets from the 1640s alone. These newssheets and pamphlets, free from censorship, soon began to carry more radical ideas – confusing, encouraging and frightening the population in equal measure. The printed word and image were being used in a way that they had never been used before.

## The end of the First Civil War

### Divisions among the Parliamentary leaders

As the last years of the First Civil War played out, Parliamentary leadership remained divided. The military failures of the Earls of Essex and Manchester, especially at the battle of Lostwithiel and the second battle of Newbury, led many, including Cromwell, to believe that they were reluctant to inflict a crushing defeat on the King. Accusations of cowardice were unfounded, but it is certain that these men were more willing to use the exhaustion of war to bring the King to a negotiated settlement. Manchester famously claimed that, 'If we beat the King ninety and nine times, yet he is King still, … and we his subjects … but if the King beat us once, we shall all be hanged'. Cromwell retorted by asking, 'If this be so, why did we ever take up arms at first?'[10]

The Self-denying Ordinance did much to exacerbate the growing divide and as the politician commanders returned to Parliament two distinct groups began to grow. The Peace Party, which saw the war in purely defensive terms, was led by men like Denzil Holles, Essex and Manchester. Their more hard-line opponents, termed the War Party, sought a permanent restriction on royal power that would be imposed by total military victory; these men included Sir Henry Vane, Sir Arthur Hesilrige and the republican Henry Marten. Although termed 'parties', these were loose collections of individuals,

**Figure 4.6:** Prince Rupert's pet dog, Boye, was a target of Parliamentarian propagandists who claimed that he was the incarnation of the Devil. Royalists adopted him as a mascot and rumours abounded that Boye would cock his leg if anyone spoke the name Pym. When Boye was killed at Marston Moor, the Parliamentarian press, who claimed the dog was a witch's familiar or the Devil in disguise, made much of his death.

### Hidden voices

## *Nehemiah Wharton*

Nehemiah Wharton was a soldier in the Earl of Essex's Parliamentary army early in the war. Soldiers saw the war as a religious mission, as a letter from Wharton confirms.

Wednesday: Mr Love gave us a famous sermon this day. Also, the soldiers brought the holy [altar] rails from Chiswick and burned them in our town. Thursday: I marched towards Uxbridge. And at Hillingdon, one mile from Uxbridge, the rails being gone, we got the surplice [priests' robes] to make us handkerchiefs; and one of the soldiers wore it to Uxbridge.[6]

and in the middle were men like Cromwell, Oliver St John and John Hampden, who pressed for military victory alongside negotiated settlement.

## Attempts at settlement

Those moderates who were keen to reach a negotiated settlement as soon as possible. These moderates saw military victories on the battlefield as a means to end – to force the other side to be ready to compromise. The trouble was that hardliners often got their way, and the lure of total military victory (which would allow a peace deal to be imposed rather than negotiated) got the better of both sides and so early peace deals were aborted.

On 2 June 1642, before the fighting had properly begun, Parliament offered the King the **Nineteen Propositions**. Buoyed up by the King's initial difficulties in raising an army and overconfident of their own military strength, Parliament's suggested peace settlement was too harsh. The lack of compromise was clear and unsurprisingly Charles dismissed the offer outright. By the beginning of 1643, however, the situation had changed and new negotiations opened in Oxford. Shocked by the King's early military successes, Parliament was willing to be more reasonable in its demands. However, discussions soon collapsed as both sides refused to let the other have control of the nation's military resources. The King's willingness to abandon these negotiations was justified by the belief that military victory was within his grasp.

By early 1645, with remodelling of the army underway and with pressure from the Scots, Parliament embarked on a fresh round of negotiations, known as the Uxbridge Propositions. Returning to a more demanding set of proposals, this settlement proposed that the King would sign the Covenant, thus agreeing to unify England and Scotland under the Presbyterian system. In addition 58 leading Royalists would be prosecuted and military officers and many civilian posts would be appointed by Parliament. With both sides confident that the coming year could see them achieve victory, the two sides reached deadlock and the Treaty of Uxbridge collapsed.

## The capture of Charles I

After Naseby in 1645 it was only a matter of time before the smaller Royalist armies, garrisons and detachments were brought to heel. Royalist attempts to recruit 10 000 troops from Ireland in return for concessions to the Irish Catholics played badly for the King when news of the negotiations with papists were leaked, and by the start of 1646 Charles's position was hopeless. In March the King sent his son, Charles, abroad to avoid capture, and a month later the King himself left his capital at Oxford, escaping through the siege lines in disguise, dressed as a servant.

Despite having been defeated, the King was reluctant to deal with the English Parliament directly, so instead he surrendered to the Scottish Covenanter army

## Voices from the past

### *Richard Baxter*

The Puritan minister Richard Baxter complained of the growing radical ideas in the army after the battle of Naseby in 1645:

… a new face of things which I never dreamt of. I heard the plotting heads [of the sectaries] very hot upon that which intimated their intention to subvert [undermine] both Church and State.[7]

### Discussion point

Why might it be surprising for a Puritan minister to be making comments like those made by Richard Baxter?

besieging Newark in the hope of persuading them over to his cause. He knew they were dissatisfied with Parliament's slow implementation of Presbyterianism in England. Having been taken north to Newcastle, for eight months the Scots Covenanters urged the King to accept the Covenant and a Presbyterian system for England. If he were to agree, they would swing their military forces against the English Parliament. But the King, considering this too great a compromise, refused. As the last Royalist garrisons surrendered across England, the war was clearly over. However, the King was still king, and there was now a peace to be won.

## Further reading

A concise yet informative overview of the First Civil War is given in Gaunt P. *The English Civil Wars, 1642–1651*. Oxford: Osprey; 2003. A more detailed yet still accessible account of the military and political developments can again be found in Smith DL. *A History of the Modern British Isles: The Double Crown, 1603–1707*. Oxford: Blackwell; 1998, or Worden B. *The English Civil Wars, 1640–1660*. London: Weidenfeld and Nicholson; 2009. A closer study of the Royalist war effort is given in Hutton R. *The Royalist War Effort, 1642–1646*. London: Routledge; 2003. p. 89 and p. 91 and Worden B. *The English Civil Wars, 1640–1660*. London: Weidenfeld and Nicholson; 2009. A detailed study of the New Model Army can be read in Roberts K. *Cromwell's War Machine: The New Model Army 1645–1660*. Barnsley, UK: Pen and Sword; 2005.

### Practice essay questions

1. 'Parliament was always likely to win the First Civil War.' Assess the validity of this view.
2. 'The creation of the New Model Army was the most significant cause of Parliamentary victory in the period 1642–46.' Assess the validity of this view.
3. 'Royalist weaknesses were more important that Parliamentary strengths in deciding the outcome of the First Civil War.' Assess the validity of this view.
4. With reference to these extracts and your understanding of the historical context, assess the value of these three sources to an historian studying the problems experienced by both sides in maintaining their war efforts.

**Extract A**

From a petition made by inhabitants of Worcestershire to the King's officials for the return of plundered horses, 1643. Worcestershire was under royalist control at this point in the war.

Upon Saturday the third of June instant we were plundered and bereft of 40 of our best horses, but as then we had not found out the authors of our said loss. Now, … we have found out our horses in the regiment of Colonel Sir Thomas Aston … But so incommiserate and unreasonable are these plunderers that (not content with the wrongful taking our said horses, beating and abusing us for only requesting to buy them again, and at their departure wilfully trooping away near a quarter of a mile over our beans and peas) but when our messengers and servant whom we employed in seeking after our horses… found them in the said regiment … the soldiers there that were possess of our said horses … did imprison and threaten our said messengers and servants and rob them … We therefore humbly beseech you that (for as much as we have made full payment of all our monthly contribution money) … we may receive such satisfaction and reparation for our wrongs as our cause requires.[11]

**Extract B**

The account of a Royalist official tasked with collecting the Excise Tax in Somerset, 1644.

[We were told by the locals] that if we would go on in the execution of our commission [ie: collecting the Excise Tax] the country would certainly drive us out with stones … The truth is we plainly discovered a practice not only to delude but oppose us, and we have good reason to believe no only Mr Kirton but many of the gentlemen of the county are privy to it by whom the people have been so animated and set against us that no man will obey us, by every man is ready to resist us … Thus have we spent more than half a year, and that remnant of our estates which we have preserved from the rebels, and yet have not done his majesty that service which perhaps may be expected from us.[12]

**Extract C**

An extract from the Royalist propaganda newspaper, *Mercurius Aulicus*, describing events in London, August 1643.

It was this day signified by letters from London, that the tumults there do daily increase, occasioned chiefly by their daily pressing men to serve in their rebellious army, seizing poor men many times in their beds, and taking them from the wife and children to fight in spite of their hearts they know not why.[13]

## Chapter summary

By the end of this chapter you should have gained a broad overview of the course of the Civil War and how the ultimate Parliamentarian victory was eventually gained. In particular, you should be able to:

- explain the significance of the strengths and weaknesses of both sides
- give reasons for the changing fortunes of war and eventual victory of Parliament
- explain the significance of the development of the New Model Army, the Self-denying Ordinance and the attempts made to reach settlement
- explain the impact of war on the general populace
- describe the role played by propagandists and publishers.

# End notes

1  The Solemn League and Covenant, quoted in Smith DL. *A History of the Modern British Isles, 1603–1707*. Oxford: Blackwell; 1998. p. 41.

2  Braddick M. *God's Fury, England's Fire: A New History of the English Civil Wars*. London: Penguin Books; 2009. p. 310

3  Quoted in Smith DL. *A History of the Modern British Isles, 1603–1707*. p. 142.

4  Purkiss D. *The English Civil War: A People's History*. London: Harper Perennial; 2007. p. 280.

5  Roberts K. *Cromwell's War Machine: The New Model Army 1645–1660*: Barnsley: Pen and Sword; 2005. p. 177.

6  The National Archives, SP 16/491/119: Wharton to George Willingham, 16 August 1642.

7  Coward B. *The Stuart Age: England 1603–1714*. London: Longman; 1994. p. 228.

8  Wilcher R. *The Writing of Royalism, 1628–1660*. Cambridge: CUP; p. 219.

9  From *Mercurius Britannicus*, 39, 10–17 June 1644. p. 303.

10  Quoted in Smith DL. *A History of the Modern British Isles, 1603–1707*. p. 143.

11  Source: British Library, Harleian Ms. 6804, f.140. Quoted in Lindley K. *The English Civil War and Revolution*. p. 57–59.

12  Source: 'Papers concerning the commissioners for excise, Somerset, November 1644, British Library, Harleian Ms. 6804', p. 284–87. Quoted in Lindley K. *The English Civil War and Revolution*. London: Routledge; 1998. p. 110–11.

13  Source: Thomas P. (ed.) *Oxford Royalist Newbooks*. London: Cornmarket Press; 1971, Vol. 1, p. 490. Quoted in Lindley K. *The English Civil War and Revolution*. p. 114.

# 5 The disintegration of the Political Nation, 1646–1649

In this section we will examine the failed attempt to reach settlement following the defeat of the King in the First Civil War. We will look into:

- Political and religious radicalism: the politicisation of the New Model Army; Lilburne and the Levellers; Fifth Monarchists; Ranters and other populist groups.
- Political and religious divisions: the attitude and actions of Charles I; divisions within the opposition to the King; the failure of attempts to reach a political settlement.
- The Second Civil War and the reasons for its outcome.
- The problem of Charles I: divisions within the army and Parliament; the trial and execution of the King.

## Introduction

In 1646, as Charles negotiated with the Scots, the final pockets of Royalist resistance surrendered. Most people believed that the final search for settlement would be decided through compromise between the English Parliament, its Scottish allies and the King himself. This final political settlement would, they thought, rebalance the constitutional arrangements between King and Parliament and return the kingdoms to a state of normality. Few had any notion of the forces of change that were about to be unleashed.

## Timeline

| 1646 | **13 July:** Newcastle Propositions presented to Charles |
|---|---|
| **1647** | **30 January:** Scots hand Charles over to Parliament<br>**March:** army petitions against proposed disbandment; Parliament issues Declaration of Dislike against petitioning by soldiers<br>**April–May:** army regiments elect 'agitators'<br>**25–27 May:** both Houses vote to disband the army<br>**3–4 June:** Cornet Joyce seizes the King for the army<br>**14 June:** General Council of the Army issues *Declaration* protesting against disbandment<br>**17 July:** General Council of the Army discusses *Heads of the Proposals*<br>**23 July:** *Heads of the Proposals* presented to Charles<br>**26 July:** rioters invade Commons in support of Presbyterian leaders; Independent minority flee to army<br>**6 August:** army occupies London and reinstates Independents<br>**15 October:** *The Case of the Army Truly Stated*<br>**28 October–5 November:** Putney Debates; *Agreement of the People* tabled<br>**11 November:** Charles escapes to the Isle of Wight<br>**24 December:** riots against Parliament's suppression of Christmas festivities<br>**26 December:** Charles concludes Engagement with Scots<br>**28 December:** Charles rejects the *Four Bills* |
| 1648 | **3 January:** Commons passes Vote of No Addresses<br>**March–July:** Rising in South Wales<br>**29 April:** army prayer meeting at Windsor Castle<br>**April–August:** rising in East Anglia<br>**May–June:** rising in Kent<br>**June–December:** rising in Yorkshire<br>**8 July:** Scots invade England in support of Charles<br>**17–19 August:** Cromwell defeats Scots at Preston; effectively ends Second Civil War<br>**24 August:** Vote of No Addresses repealed<br>**18 September:** Treaty of Newport begins<br>**20 November:** *Remonstrance of the Army* presented to Parliament<br>**30 November:** *Declaration of the Army*<br>**2 December:** army re-enters London<br>**5 December:** Commons votes by 129 to 83 to continue negotiations with Charles<br>**6 December:** Pride's Purge |
| 1649 | **6 January:** Rump establishes High Court of Justice to try Charles<br>**20 January:** Charles's trial opens in Westminster Hall<br>**27 January:** Charles sentenced to death<br>**30 January:** Charles executed |

# Political and religious radicalism

## The politicisation of the New Model Army

In theory the army was the tool of its political masters in Parliament at Westminster. However, the army began to grow in self-confidence and political awareness, ensuring it became a major political player in its own right. It did so for two reasons; first because of its practical grievances, and second, because of a growing culture of religious and political radicalism among its soldiers.

## Practical grievances of the army

As the fighting ended, three practical issues concerned the army. The first was that before being disbanded the soldiers should receive their arrears of pay; some estimates place these as high as £3 million. Second, the army was keen to secure indemnity from arrest for war crimes committed in the service of Parliament's cause. The line between lawful **requisitioning** of goods and plunder in wartime had been blurred and the last thing soldiers wanted was to face criminal charges for deeds they had committed during the war. Finally, the soldiers sought a guarantee that they would not be forced to serve abroad or in Ireland. These concerns have been rightly labelled 'bread-and-butter' issues for they did not contain political demands.[1] However, Parliament's refusal to address the army's grievances meant that the army was forced to develop a voice of its own. Once established, this voice would easily begin to assert political views on the search for settlement and the shape it should take.

The reluctance of MPs to listen to the army's grievances was, to a degree, understandable. The cost of the army was crippling. Conscious that wartime assessments far exceeded those raised during the 'tyranny' of the Personal Rule, MPs sought to bring this to an end as soon as possible; disbandment of the army must come first, and they argued that it was far more pressing than satisfying the army's grievances. By the spring of 1647 the army had prepared a petition that would be presented to their commander, Sir Thomas Fairfax, urging redress of their grievances. This army petition enraged many conservative MPs who favoured a settlement along Presbyterian lines (see the section on Divisions within the opposition to the King). These Presbyterian MPs, led by Denzil Holles, dominated the Derby House Committee (a parliamentary committee that increasingly drove policy at this point) and pushed forward plans to send some regiments to bring order to Ireland, disband the remainder and raise a small standing army whose officers were willing to conform to the Presbyterian system. This small force would be based not on the New Model regiments but on the London Trained Bands that formed the London militia. Their disdain for the New Model Army was revealed in the Declaration of Dislike passed in March 1647, which labelled petitions from the army as treasonable. This was a grave misjudgement, for the Declaration of Dislike alienated the very men who had gained victory in the First Civil War and only spurred on the soldiers to pursue their aims. In April and May the regiments began to elect individual soldiers as 'agitators' to represent their views in council with senior officers. The army was finding its voice.

With growing mutinous feeling in the army, Holles and the Presbyterian faction in Parliament were heartened by the King's willingness to consider a Presbyterian settlement as a basis for negotiations. There was no longer any need for an army and so on 25 May MPs voted to disband all infantry regiments, paying them only eight weeks' wage arrears. In response to this flagrant disregard for the army's well-being Fairfax ordered a general rendezvous of the army at Newmarket. The transformation of the army into a fully-fledged political entity was not long in coming. On 2 June 1647 a junior officer, Cornet Joyce, and his troop of cavalry arrived at Holdenby House in Northamptonshire where the King was under house arrest. Joyce seized the King from the parliamentary commissioners at Holdenby and took him east to join the rendezvous of the army at Newmarket. On 5 June, in a document titled *A Solemn Engagement,* the army declared its refusal to disband until its grievances had been met. In seizing the King the army had become a political force in its own right and was able to influence all future negotiations.

On 14 June when discussions between agitators and officers, now known as the General Council of the Army, produced a *Declaration*, it was clear that material

---

### Key term

**requisitioning:** the forceful confiscation of goods, often by armies grievances had developed into a political view. The *Declaration* stated that it was 'not a mere mercenary army' but one that had a political agenda dedicated to 'the defence of our own and the people's just rights and liberties'. The text of the *Declaration* laid out the army's desire to see the present Parliament purged of Holles's Presbyterian faction, that future parliaments would only sit for a fixed period, a guaranteed right of a subject to petition Parliament, and that any religious settlement would allow a degree of freedom for people to follow their 'tender consciences' and not just conform to a national church.

### A growing culture of religious and political radicalism

Parliament's unwillingness to address soldiers' grievances was pivotal in turning the army into a political force. However, there is a strong argument to suggest that religious radicalism spurred it on. The New Model Army was known for its religious zeal and there were many Puritans within its ranks. In fighting the First Civil War they had hoped to purge the Church of the last remnants of the old Catholic faith. Puritan soldiers had a strong desire to see the final peace settlement with the King reflect the reasons they had taken up arms in the first place.

But for others in the army, this was not enough, as the references to religious toleration in the army *Declaration* of 14 June showed. Religious extremism was now going beyond the limits of Puritanism. In the army and society more generally what became known as the 'gathered churches' began to emerge. In the void left by the absence of bishops and the collapse of censorship, a variety of religious congregations had begun to appear. These congregations sought freedom from an established state Church and were often referred to as **'Dissenters'** as a result. Dissenters looked to worship God in the manner they saw fit (see Table 5.1). Puritan critics who still believed in the need for a reformed national Church went so far as to describe these congregations as a 'canker', or cancer, that threatened to eat away the body of the Church. Thus, while Puritans within the army might have disagreed with their more radical comrades over the role of a state church, the foundation of religious radicalism within the army was leading to more powerfully expressed political views.

The willingness of the army to assert a political voice was reinforced by the common belief in Providence – that the will of God would be revealed in events on Earth. This led many radicals who dissented from a state Church to interpret the upheaval of civil war as the embodiment of God's will – a cataclysmic struggle between the forces of good and evil that was destined to end with God's victory and the 1000-year rule of King Jesus and the Saints. This belief, also known as **millenarianism**, saw the creation of small separatist congregations who declined to follow any national church (see Table 5.1). Throughout the war and in the months following it the army sheltered and assisted these fellow radicals in establishing or maintaining separatist congregations. Indeed, Cromwell's personal belief in people's right to worship God as they wished, or **'liberty of conscience'** as he called it, was reflective of broader attitudes in the army. Many agitators wanted the army to have a political voice so that they could make their views on religious issues heard in the final peace settlement. In the summer of 1647, the General Council of the Army produced a new peace offer to the King. Drafted largely by two senior commanders, Cromwell and his son-in-law Henry Ireton, and presented to the King on 23 July, the *Heads of Proposals* was perhaps the clearest sign that the army was now a political force.

## Lilburne and the Levellers

Radicalism was not easy to contain, and as the summer and autumn of 1647 progressed, pockets within the army began to become more extreme in their political beliefs. This was largely due to the influence of the Levellers, led by John Lilburne, Richard Overton and William Walwyn (see the sections on The strengths and weaknesses of the political and military leadership of the Parliamentary forces and

### ACTIVITY 5.1

Read the section on The politicisation of the New Model Army and using the headings '**Date**', '**Parliament's actions**' and '**Army's actions**' create a timeline of actions that shows how this politicisation developed.

### Key term

**Dissenters:** name given to people who refused to follow the rules of the established Church. They dissented from the doctrine the Church laid down and conducted worship and services in their own ways.

### Key term

**millenarianism:** the belief that the thousand year reign of King Jesus and 'the saints' (godly people) was imminent. Many millenarians saw the upheaval of civil war as indicative of the impending return of Christ.

### Key term

**liberty of conscience:** the idea that people should be free to follow their own beliefs in worshipping God. This implied weakening the power of the state Church and the end of compulsory church attendance. It generally referred to non-Catholic denominations.

| | Outline of beliefs |
|---|---|
| Baptists (also known as Anabaptists) | One of the religious denominations that made up the 'gathered churches' following the First Civil War. Baptists rejected the idea that people were predestined to go to either heaven or hell, but instead believed that human beings could earn their place in heaven through good deeds and turning their back on sin. Adult baptisms were symbolic of this ability to purify the human soul. |
| Fifth Monarchists | Saw the cataclysmic upheaval embodied in the civil war and the Thirty Years' War in Europe as a precursor to the second coming of Christ. They believed that that the 1000-year rule of 'King Jesus and the Saints' (godly people) was imminent and that the nation should be prepared. |
| Independents or Congregationalists | Protestants who disliked the Church of England. They believed that congregations should worship in the form they thought best, free from the control of bishops and prayer books. They distrusted Presbyterianism just as much as Anglicanism. |
| Quakers | Believed in a personal relationship with God through the teachings of Christ. They rejected the idea of an organised clergy and instead maintained that all believers were priests of the Church. Close study of the Bible was a hallmark of their followers. Quakers refused to conform to social norms or to swear oaths. Only in the years after the Restoration did they become famed for their pacifism and opposition to war. |
| Seekers | Rejected all forms of organised religion and instead sought the revelation of God's will. They saw formal Church structures and priests as corrupt. Like the Quakers they placed great emphasis on Bible study. Following the civil war many Seekers joined the Quakers. |
| Ranters | Believed that God resided in every living thing and therefore there was no need for social hierarchy. As a result they rejected all conventions of manners and public decency. As they were chosen by God they felt it was impossible for them to sin. They became known for moral outrages, public obscenities and promiscuous sexual activity. |
| Muggletonians | An obscure group. Their beliefs centred on the idea that God only existed when he appeared in the form of man as Jesus Christ. Sin was seen not as an offence against God, but against human conscience and humankind's ability to reason. |

**Table 5.1:** The variety of religious sects.

### ACTIVITY 5.2

In what ways did the radical sects described in Table 5.1 pose a threat to social order?

### Key term

**suffrage:** the right to vote. Universal male suffrage referred to the right of all men to vote in elections for Parliament.

The emergence of the New Model Army in Chapter 4). Between 1642 and 1644 Lilburne had been a soldier in the Parliamentarian army, fighting in the regiment led by Lord Brooke, a well-known champion of religious liberty. However, Lilburne left the army in 1645 when he refused to swear to the Solemn League and Covenant because it required England to adopt Presbyterianism. He was nicknamed 'Freeborn John'.

Although the Leveller leaders differed in their religious beliefs, they all agreed that toleration was the only way forward. What was new about their views, however, was the belief that the liberties of the English people went beyond simple religious tolerance and extended to full-scale political and social reform. Lilburne had himself been in trouble with the authorities during the Personal Rule when he had assisted in the publication of one of Bastwick's anti-Laudian pamphlets. The historian Barry Coward has noted that the titles of these pamphlets reveal much about people's political beliefs, for example *England's Lamentable Slaverie* (published by Walwyn in October 1645), *An Arrow Against all Tyrants* (published by Overton in October 1646) and *London's Liberty in Chains* (published by Lilburne in November 1646). The main aims of these pamphleteers were to return citizens to a state of liberty, which they considered to be the right of all freeborn English people. In real terms this meant a total overhaul of existing structures that had become corrupted by greedy and powerful elites within society and included abolition of the monarchy and the House of Lords, an end to the Church of England, the creation of a single-chamber parliament elected by universal male **suffrage** and regular elections once every one or two years.

To the majority of people at the time such views must have appeared horrific, promising yet more upheaval and disturbance of normality. But to many discontented soldiers in the army, feeling betrayed by their political masters in Westminster, such ideas seemed attractive. The Levellers seemed to be the only people to see the situation for what it was: in their negotiations with the King MPs were slowly ensuring a Presbyterian future for England; army generals like Cromwell and Ireton were being duped by the King's apparent willingness to negotiate: and all the while the great achievements gained on the battlefield were being squandered. It is hard to determine how many within the army held Leveller beliefs but their ideas certainly became widely distributed in 'a series of scorching pamphlets hot from presses hidden in the quarters of sympathetic soldiers, who subscribed four pence (half their daily wage) to pay for the print and for its delivery to regiments in other parts of the army'.[2]

The Leveller influence within the army reached its zenith in October 1647 when the more radical agitators from five regiments drew up *The Case of the Army Truly Stated*, which attacked the General Council of the Army for being too soft in its approach and asserted the idea that all power was derived from the people of the nation. Having decided to meet Leveller representatives to discuss the document, the General Council of the Army was shocked to discover an even more revolutionary document tabled by the Levellers, *The Agreement of the People* (see the section on The failure of attempts to reach a political settlement later in this chapter).

## Fifth Monarchists

As we saw earlier in this chapter, millenarianism was the broad belief that the 1000-year rule of 'King Jesus and the Saints' would follow a cataclysmic struggle between the forces of good and evil on Earth. For many, the civil war was part of this struggle. The Fifth Monarchists were a religious group that took millenarian belief a step further and believed that the second coming of Christ and his subsequent reign were imminent. They took their belief and name from the prophesy of Nebuchadnezzar's dream recorded in the Old Testament of the Bible that the fifth monarchy of Christ's kingdom would come about after the collapse of four other kingdoms. All that could be done to make England ready for Christ's second coming should be done, not by elected parliaments, but rather by themselves, 'who as God's elect would subjugate the wicked'.[4]

Like the Levellers, The Fifth Monarchists were happy to see the political and social order turned on its head. Where they differed was in believing that all power should rest with God's elect – the godly 'saints' as they saw themselves.[5] They too found supporters within the army, many from more humble backgrounds who had risen to senior ranks. Typical of these was Thomas Harrison, a son of the mayor of Newcastle-under-Lyme, who rose to the rank of Major-General. For some time Harrison and the Fifth Monarchists enjoyed a degree of sympathy from Cromwell who respected their godly zeal. However, much of the hostility aimed at radical groups like the

---

**ACTIVITY 5.3**

Read *The Case of the Army Truly Stated* in Voices from the past, and complete the tasks below.

1. Summarise the points being made by the Levellers in this document.
2. Why did they feel justified in stating their views?
3. Why would many MPs have been shocked by this document?

---

### Voices from the past

## *The Case of the Army Truly Stated, 1648*

The grievances, dissatisfactions and desires of the army, both as commoners and soldiers, has been many months since represented to the Parliament, and the army has waited with much patience to see their common grievances redressed and the rights and freedoms of the nation cleared and secured;
… We propound [that] … all power is originally and essentially in the whole body of the people of this nation, and whereas their free choice or consent by their representers is the only original or foundation of all just government.[3]

**ACTIVITY 5.4**

Why do you think the publishers of *The Ranters Ranting* used an image as well as text to convey their message?

Fifth Monarchists derived from their humble backgrounds. One contemporary described them as 'the worst of men, the scum and very froth of baseness'.[6]

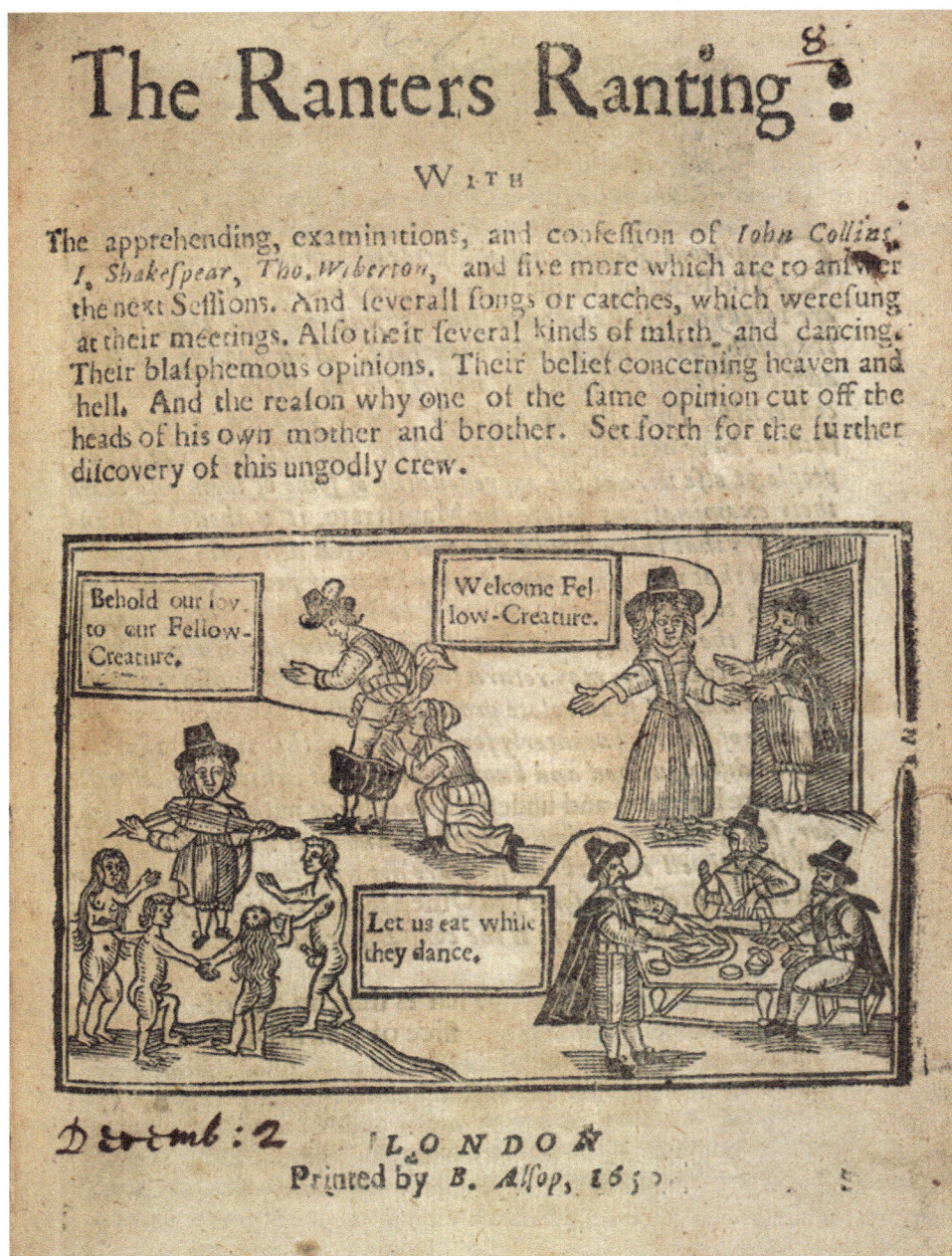

**Figure 5.1:** The Ranters, like the other radical sects, produced a strong response from more conservative opinion.

## Ranters and other populist groups

Any chance of returning to familiar normality was further threatened by the development of a plethora of extremist groups, or sectaries, as they became known. The Ranters, as their name suggests, were unreasonable religious fundamentalists who believed that their special bond with God freed them from all moral conventions. They maintained that sin was a creation of the human mind and because God resided in all living things, inspiring their actions, no laws or codes were needed and anything was permitted. They had no clear leader, and their small membership, among the rural and urban poor, is hard to quantify. Nonetheless stories abounded about their morally degenerate actions and women stripping naked in church claiming to be impregnated by God; indeed nudity was a common feature of their social protest.

The conservative pamphlets that damned the actions of the Ranters reveal the popular fear that the world as people knew it was collapsing about their ears. Figure 5.1 reproduces the cover of a conservative pamphlet against the Ranters that claims to expose their meetings at which songs were sung, '[a]lso several kings of mirth [amusement] and dancing. Their blasphemous opinions. Their belief concerning heaven and hell. And the reason why one of the same opinion cut off the heads of his own mother and brother. Set forth for the further discovery of this ungodly crew'.[7] The prominent role played by women in the radical sects reinforced conservative concerns. In the Leveller movement, for example, leaders' wives were active in petitioning on behalf of their imprisoned husbands, whereas female Ranters broke away from the sexual and moral conventions of the period.

The radical groups outlined in Table 5.1 emerged at a time when the Church of England was in flux and the future seemed uncertain. Radical groups split opinion, deepened concerns, and ultimately led to an upsurge in conservative feeling and sympathy for the King.

# Political and religious divisions

## The attitude and actions of Charles I

The King had hoped that by surrendering to the Scots in 1646 he would be able to reach a deal with them directly, splitting his opponents and then turning their military force against his rebellious Parliament. There was some merit in this approach because many in the Scottish ranks felt that the English experiment of introducing Presbyterianism into the Church of England had been half-hearted. Charles's broader aim, to play his opponents off against each other, meant that all he needed to do was sit tight and wait for the best deal. However, Charles waited too long to play his hand and failed to accept any of the deals offered to him. His opponents began to fear that he was being deceitful, spinning out time and only pretending to consider their proposals. Charles also continued to harbour hopes of renewing a military campaign against his opponents. This was another critical mistake because when he finally made his move, and it failed, it reinforced the idea that Charles could not be trusted.

Between May 1646 and January 1647 the Scots in Newcastle urged Charles to accept a Presbyterian settlement but he made no agreements and instead played for time. On 13 July 1646 Parliamentary commissioners travelled north to present him with the Newcastle Propositions. These required Charles to accept the Solemn League and Covenant, the sale of one-third of land owned by bishops and the clergy, Parliament to have sole control over the armed forces for the next 20 years (the assumed lifespan of the King) and 58 leading Royalists to be barred from office and eligible for prosecution. Again, Charles delayed, hoping that either the Scots or Parliament would break the deadlock by offering a better deal. Eventually, with Parliament using a loan of £230 000 from the City of London to pay off the Scottish army, Charles was handed over to Parliament and the Scots returned home. Under house arrest at Holdenby House in Northamptonshire, Charles continued discussions with the Parliamentary commissioners.

The growing gulf between Parliament and the army vindicated his decision to sit tight and watch his opponents turn on each other. In June 1647, when Cornet Joyce seized the King from his Parliamentary captors at Holdenby, Charles was willing enough to

**ACTIVITY 5.5**

1. Why did Charles decide to reject the peace settlements offered to him?

2. Why was it reasonable to think that this strategy would prove successful?

3. Why was rejection of the peace settlements a high-risk strategy?

go and must have been satisfied with the result. Even though radical voices in the army were growing louder the peace settlement the army presented to the King in July 1647, titled the *Heads of the Proposals,* was far more lenient than Parliament's Newcastle Propositions. The key differences were that bishops were allowed to remain (although with highly restricted powers), that the Book of Common Prayer would remain but be used only on a voluntary basis, the Triennial Act would be repealed in favour of biennial parliaments, ministers would be appointed by the King but with parliamentary approval and the armed forces would be controlled by Parliament for 10 rather than 20 years. In addition, only seven leading Royalists would be denied a pardon and others would only be debarred from holding office for five years.

This was to be the most lenient settlement Charles was to be offered. Charles, however, believed that it was a sign that his strategy was working and instead he decided to wait and see if Parliament would offer an even better deal. Charles remained rooted to the belief that he was answerable only to God and that he should not do anything to compromise the royal authority of either himself or his successors. In hindsight it is perhaps easy to criticise Charles for not accepting the *Heads of the Proposals*; however, the longer time dragged on the more people's sympathies seemed to be siding with the King. Charles was increasingly being seen as the victim whereas Parliament was seen as divided and vindictive; the army, on the other hand, seemed to be a hotbed of radical sectaries. And so Charles continued to gamble.

## Divisions within the opposition to the King

Following the war, two distinct sides emerged in Parliament. The Presbyterians, led by Denzil Holles, counted the Earl of Essex, William Strode and Sir Philip Stapleton among their number, and grew out of the wartime Peace Party, which had favoured a negotiated settlement. These men tended towards a more conservative settlement along broadly Presbyterian lines with severely restricted powers for bishops and a close alliance with the Scots as the best chance for order and stability. In their eyes the King was now free of his evil advisors and should be a major element in the settlement process. It is probably fair to say that their conservative outlook reflected the popular view of many English men and women who favoured a return to normality as soon as possible.

The Independent faction, which emerged from the more aggressive War Party, shared a desire for the return to normality but more pressing for them was the desire to provide for liberty of conscience. They certainly wanted a stable church but also wanted space for freedom of worship and 'independent' congregations. The Independents, including Viscount Saye and Sele, Oliver St John, Sir Arthur Hesilrige and Oliver Cromwell, were hostile to an intolerant Presbyterian settlement. The *Heads of the Proposals* show that in the years that followed the war they were willing to go a long way to compromise with Charles. Unlike the Presbyterians, the Independents found common ground with the New Model Army, not least because their religious outlook seemed to give hope for toleration of more radical views.

The various clashes between the army and Parliament had led the army to seize the King. To demonstrate its newly acquired political voice on 14 June the General Army Council had issued a *Declaration* that outlined not only its practical grievances but also asserted that it stood for 'the people's just rights and liberties'. As if to echo some the calls of some of the Leveller agitators, the *Declaration* defended the right of petitioning as the right of 'all free-born people', stressed the need to provide provision for tender consciences and called for a dissolution of Parliament and fresh elections.[8] Worried that he and the Presbyterians were losing the initiative to the army and their Independent allies in Parliament, on 26 July Holles encouraged a violent mob to invade the Commons in support of his party. In the short term it seemed to succeed as over 50 Independent MPs fled Westminster for the protection of the army, which was now encamped at St Albans. However, Holles's success was short-lived and on 6 August the New Model Army occupied London and as Holles and 10 leading Presbyterians fled the capital the Independent MPs were reinstated.

## The failure of attempts to reach a political settlement

Seeing divisions emerge between Parliament and the army, and then within Parliament itself, the King had hoped for a more favourable offer from one of the rival groups, and in this at least he was proved right. In July 1647 the army had presented the *Heads of the Proposals* and by August 1647, with their Independent allies dominating Parliament, it seemed as though the army's proposals might stand some chance of being accepted by the King. With the King now held at Hampton Court Palace on the outskirts of London, and the army encamped nearby in the town of Putney, discussions between the King and his captors continued. Once again, Charles played for time.

Frustrated at the drawn-out negotiations, radical Levellers had drawn up the document *The Case of the Army Truly Stated,* criticising the General Council of the Army. Eager to prevent the Leveller influence getting out of control, the socially conservative generals Cromwell and Ireton (or the grandees, as they became known) arranged for the General Council to meet the agitators at Putney church to discuss the document. The Putney debates lasted from 28 October to 5 November 1647 and on the first day the grandees found themselves confronted by an even more radical Leveller document entitled *The Agreement of the People.* This went further than the *Case of the Army Truly Stated,* arguing for the abolition of the monarchy, universal male suffrage and total equality before the law. These ideas were remarkably ahead of their time and would not be voiced in France, for example, for another century. While the Levellers argued that all freemen should have a say in who ruled the country (see Voices from the Past: Colonel Rainsborough and General Henry Ireton) Cromwell and Ireton reflected the conservative outlook of the gentry. They stressed that any future settlement would require the King's involvement and more importantly that the social order should be maintained. Ireton believed that Leveller ideas would 'end in anarchy', stating that only men of property who had a 'permanent fixed interest in the nation' deserved the right to elect MPs. By 5 November the discussions had become so radical in nature that Cromwell ordered the clerks to stop taking minutes of the discussions and the debates ended with no clear outcome. Cromwell decided that three rendezvous of different regiments would help reunite the army and re-establish the authority of the General Council. However, at the first of these on 15 November Cromwell narrowly avoided a mutiny when men of one of the regiments appeared with copies of *The Agreement of the People* stuffed into their hats. In a show of personal bravery Cromwell and his officers rode through the troops snatching up the documents and then had one of the ringleaders summarily tried and shot as an example.

In the end, however, events overtook such theoretical debates, for on 11 November news reached Cromwell that the King had escaped from Hampton Court Palace in an attempt to enter negotiations with the Scots. A second civil war was looming.

## The Second Civil War and the reasons for its outcome

Charles's decision to escape from Hampton Court in November 1647 was the first step towards the renewal of military conflict in what has been termed the Second Civil War. Charles fled to Carisbrooke Castle on the Isle of Wight where he understood the Governor, Colonel Hammond, was sympathetic to his plight. This was not the case and Hammond soon informed Parliament that he was holding Charles in custody on the island. However, this did not prevent Charles from brokering a treaty with the Scots, known as the Engagement. Agreed on 26 December 1647, The Engagement saw Charles finally promise to introduce Scottish Presbyterianism to England on an experimental basis in return for military aid.

ACTIVITY 5.6

Read the section the Second Civil War.

1. Why did Charles feel confident in launching a second Civil War?

2. Create a mind map showing all the reasons why the Royalists and Scots lost the Second Civil War.

3. Which reasons do you think were most significant? Why?

Such a gamble could be seen as foolhardy, not least as the agreement over Presbyterianism was a considerably worse settlement than that offered in the *Heads of the Proposals*. However, Charles's confidence was not totally unfounded. The divisions between the army and Parliament, the clash between the Independents and Presbyterians, and the added pressure of the Levellers and other radical sects was causing widespread anxiety among the people. The ongoing burden of taxation caused anger and the inability of the victors to win the peace was reason enough to swing people's sympathy behind the King. Charles's confidence was boosted by negotiations with Irish leaders who were dissatisfied with Parliament's handling of Irish affairs. Thus, the chance of stimulating pro-Royalist uprisings across England and Wales, coupled with the invasion of England by a Scottish (and possibly an Irish) army, made the gamble seem worthwhile. A show of force, Charles thought, would show that he was now in the dominant position and would allow him to dictate terms of settlement. Charles rejected Parliament's final settlement, the *Four Bills* (see Table 5.2), confident that the military campaign to follow would turn the tables in his favour.

The Second Civil War was something of a military disaster for Charles. Although he may have been heartened by the riots, risings and rebellions that spread across the country in the spring of 1648 they were disjointed and sporadic. Some supported Royalism, whereas others were a response to local issues. In southwest Wales the risings were more serious. In one case, disillusioned parliamentarian troops commanded by Colonel John Poyer mutinied against arrears of pay and then, with their ranks swollen by disbanded soldiers, declared their support for the King.

Lacking any central co-ordination or clear command structures, many of these risings either fizzled out or were crushed by local forces. There were, however, some more serious challenges. The first arose in Kent in May and June 1648. Dispatching Cromwell to deal with the Welsh risings, Fairfax dealt with the Kentish rebels himself. After an abortive Royalist attempt to threaten London, Fairfax pursued the Royalists into Essex where he laid siege to Colchester. The fighting was brutal and when the starving Royalist garrison finally surrendered in August its commanders were summarily executed. At the same time Cromwell marched west to deal with the Welsh rebels. By the time he arrived, local forces had already had some success and so Cromwell

## Voices from the past

### Colonel Rainsborough and General Henry Ireton at the Putney Debates, 1647

The Levellers who attended the Putney Debates with the General Council of the Army were drawn from all ranks. In a expression of true equality the Leveller agitator Sexby, an ordinary soldier from the ranks, was supported by Colonel Rainsborough. The following quote from Rainsborough's speech is reflective of the core message of the Leveller movement. While it seems akin to modern views of democracy and freedom, it must have seemed shocking to those who felt that political freedom was the preserve of men of property.

The poorest he that is in England hath a life to live as the greatest he; and therefore truly, sir, I think it clear that every man that is to live under a government ought first by his own consent to put himself under that government; and I do think that the poorest man in England is not at all bound in a strict sense to that government that he has not had a voice to put himself under; I am confident that when I have heard the reasons against it, something will be said to answer those reasons.[9]

Henry Ireton's response reflects the conservative outlook of the grandees.

No person hath a right to an interest or share in the disposing of the affairs of the kingdom, and in determining or choosing those that shall determine what laws we shall be ruled by here – no person hath a right to this, that hath not a permanent fixed interest in this kingdom.[10]

mopped up the Royalists who held Chepstow Castle, Tenby and Pembroke Castle. Their commanders drew lots, and the unlucky Colonel John Poyer was taken to London and executed.

When the Duke of Hamilton, commanding the Scottish army, finally invaded, the English and Welsh risings were nearing their end. Having defeated the Welsh Royalists, Cromwell marched north. Hamilton's army had already been weakened by General Leslie's refusal to join the invasion and so were no match for Cromwell, who was able to out-manoeuvre them. He cut their line of supplies, inflicted a crushing defeat at the battle of Preston on 17 August and won a series of smaller engagements in the days that followed. Although the navy had mutinied in favour of the King this counted for little without success on land, and so the Second Civil War effectively came to an end.

> ### Taking it further
>
> Read Diane Purkiss's chapter on the Second Civil War in her book *The English Civil War: A People's History* (p. 532–42).[11] What does it reveal about:
>
> 1. Reasons for Royalist and Scottish defeat?
> 2. The severity of the fighting and the impact this had on people's opinions?

## The problem of Charles I

### Divisions within the army and Parliament

The Second Civil War shifted attitudes, particularly in the army. To those who sought signs of God's Providence in worldly events, a second defeat for the King seemed to indicate that his cause was truly damned. At the same time, his Engagement with the Scots and their invasion of England was a sign of duplicity and dishonesty. For the army it now seemed clear why previous negotiations had failed – the King had never intended to reach a compromise. This new attitude united the views of both officers and men and was revealed in the Windsor prayer meeting held by officers at the end of April 1648. The conclusion they reached at this meeting was that the King, or 'Charles Stuart' as they now disdainfully referred to him, was guilty of deceit over the *Heads of the Proposals*. In wilfully waging war for a second time, Charles Stuart had proved beyond doubt that he was a 'man of blood', unworthy of his sacred and regal position as king. In the Bible, in texts such as Numbers (35: 33) they found guidance on how to deal with such men: 'Blood it defileth the land: and the land cannot be cleansed of the blood that is shed therein, but by the blood of him that shed it'. Such a shift in attitudes would, in the fullness of time, prove decisive; but in the short term it came to guide the army's brutality in crushing the Royalist uprisings and their interactions with Parliament.

To begin with, Parliament responded to the King's Engagement with the Scots with a disdain equal to that of the army. On 3 January 1648 Parliament had passed the Vote of No Addresses, which effectively ended all negotiations with Charles. However, by the end of August, with the Royalists and Scots defeated, Parliament voted to open negotiations once more, this time at Newport. The King agreed to parliamentary control of the militia but he remained obstinate over the issue of bishops – he was willing to suspend the episcopacy for three years but made clear he would revoke this concession as soon as possible.

For the army this was a gross betrayal of all they had fought for. This time Ireton led the army by drafting an army petition, the *Remonstrance*, which was presented to Parliament on 20 November. It called for the 'capital and grand author of all our troubles' to be brought to justice, for the Long Parliament to be dissolved in favour of fresh elections on a wide **franchise** with the power to elect a new monarch if it saw fit. The army was clearly after vengeance against Charles Stuart and when Parliament simply ignored the Remonstrance, the army's patience was sorely tested. It finally broke when on 5 December 1648 MPs voted to accept the King's responses at the Newport negotiations as appropriate grounds upon which to continue negotiations. The army was now totally at odds with Parliament and action was deemed necessary.

On the morning of 6 December Britain experienced a **military coup d'état**. As MPs arrived at Westminster they were met by Colonel Thomas Pride and his regiment. In what became known as 'Pride's Purge', 45 MPs who had voted to continue negotiations with the King were arrested, 186 were barred entry to the Commons and 86 more withdrew in protest or fear. The remaining MPs, about 150 in number, more radical in outlook and sympathetic to the army's position, were allowed to sit and formed what became known as the 'Rump Parliament'. This 'Rump' of MPs gave the army's actions a thin veil of parliamentary legitimacy, though many saw it for what it really was, a military coup. Cromwell, heading south from his victory over the Scots, arrived in London on the evening of 6 December, with Pride's Purge complete. Although it is likely that he knew of the plan to purge Parliament he was either reluctant to be associated with this gross breach of parliamentary privilege, or was clever enough to distance himself from the action. Either way, the path was now clear to bring Charles to trial.

## The trial and execution of the King

In the last days of 1648 Cromwell made one last attempt to reach conciliation with the King via the Earl of Denbigh (see Taking it further). When Charles remained unwilling to deal with what he considered to be an unlawful power, the 'Denbigh mission' failed and Cromwell resolved to 'cut off the King's head with the Crown upon it'. On 1 January 1649 the Commons passed an ordinance that established a High Court of Justice to sit in judgement on the King. The House of Lords, aware of how revolutionary this step was, refused to pass it, whereupon the Commons simply bypassed the Lords, asserting that they were the supreme power in the nation. The Rump used this authority to establish a High Court of Justice made up of 135 MPs, officers and civilians, headed by John Bradshaw, a provincial judge and a known republican.

The charges levelled at the King (see Voices from the past: The charge made against the King during his trial, 1649) held him personally responsible for the horrors and bloodshed of the civil wars, impeaching him as 'a tyrant, traitor and murderer, and a public and implacable enemy to the Commonwealth of England'.[12] Charles, well versed in legal matters, laughed at the charges and refused to plead. In one of the finest performances of his reign, Charles spoke without stammer or hesitation, setting himself up as a champion of the people's rights. He invoked Biblical commandments of the need to obey kings, the Common Law principle that 'the King could do no wrong', and his coronation oath 'to defend the fundamental laws of [the] kingdom'. Most powerfully, in claiming that the court constituted a power rather than a lawful authority, he asked what chance any other freeborn English person would have for a fair trial if he, the King, was denied one. Because he refused to recognise the legitimacy of the court and to enter a plea, Charles was denied the right to speak further. On 27 January 1649 the court found him guilty of treason against 'the good people of this nation'. But for all the legal pretence, there was no hiding the dubious legality of the trial. Of the 135 members of the High Court only 59 agreed to sign the death warrant, one of the notable exceptions being Sir Thomas Fairfax who felt that the army had gone too far in the matter. It is rumoured that when the clerk at the trial asked his whereabouts, Lady Fairfax called from the public gallery, 'He has more wit than to be here'.[13]

This revolutionary act was driven by a small minority of men, behind whom stood the army. However, what is less clear is whether the death of the King was a foregone conclusion. More recently historians have suggested that the trial was not merely a charade intended to legitimise **regicide**, but rather an attempt to force the King into reaching a settlement on the army's terms. These arguments suggest that the charges were so flimsy that the King could easily have pleaded not guilty and defended his person, shifting the guilt elsewhere. In entering a plea he would have acknowledged the legitimacy of the army-backed High Court to negotiate. In the end, it mattered little, for by refusing to plead on a point of legal principle – that the Court was not legitimate – Charles called its bluff, sealed his fate and ensured that only one outcome could be reached. If it had been one last attempt at reconciliation, it failed dramatically.

On the morning of 30 January 1649, Charles I donned two shirts for fear that if he shivered in the cold morning air his trembling would be taken for fear. With admirable courage, he stepped out of a second-floor window of the Banqueting House at Whitehall on to a temporary scaffold that was draped all in black. One of his last sights before confronting the assembled crowd must have been the Rubens ceiling that depicted his father rising to heaven and becoming a god. Evidently inspired, he spoke clearly, without his usual stammer, and decried the abuse of military power; he asserted that he died a Christian death, as a martyr for the cause of liberty and the freedom of his subjects. These were no empty words and did more to reaffirm popular faith in monarchy than anything Charles had done in life. If the actions of the crowd on that fateful morning were anything to go by, Charles's message struck home – many spoke of a dreadful moan rising from the crowd as the King's head was severed; some fainted with shock and others, in an expression of the lasting belief in the divine nature of monarchy, dipped their handkerchiefs in the blood that dripped from the scaffold, convinced of its supernatural power to cure illness (see Figure 5.2). The King was dead but England's woes had still to be settled.

### Key term

**regicide:** the act of killing a monarch. The word is derived from the Latin word *regis*, meaning 'of the king'.

### Voices from the past

#### *The charge made against the King during his trial, 1649*

That the said Charles Stuart, … out of a wicked design to erect and uphold in himself an unlimited and tyrannical power to rule according to his will, and to overthrow the rights and liberties of the people … [and] hath been, and is the occasioner, author, and continuer of the said unnatural, cruel and bloody wars; and therein guilty of all the treasons, murders, rapines, burnings, spoils, desolations, damages and mischiefs to this nation, acted and committed in the said wars, or occasioned thereby.[14]

**Figure 5.2:** This stylised depiction of Charles's execution highlights the lasting impression the King was able to make on the people.

Within days of the axe severing Charles's head from his body, copies of *Eikon Basilike*, a supposed collection of Charles's speeches and meditations, flooded the nation and established the image of Charles the martyr king. In the years that followed the execution, the *Eikon Basilike* appeared in 36 editions. It did much to rally popular sympathy for the Royalist cause and in the long term, that sympathy would translate into support for the restoration of Charles II in 1660.

## Further reading

An excellent overview of the period can once again be found in Smith DL. *A History of the Modern British Isles, 1603–1707*. Oxford: Blackwell; 1998. Diane Purkiss's *The English Civil War: A People's History*. London: Harper Perennial; 2007 also gives an enlightening view of events from the perspective of contemporaries and there is a detailed analysis of the Levellers and their demands, reproducing many key primary texts, in Robertson G. *The Levellers: The Putney Debates*. London; Verso; 2007.

**Figure 5.3:** The frontispiece of *Eikon Basilike*. The popularity of this publication reveals the underlying sympathy that people felt for the dead King and their hostility to the Army and Rump for carrying out the regicide.

### Practice essay questions

1. 'The failure to reach settlement in the years 1646–48 was largely due to the politicisation of the army.' Assess the validity of this view.
2. 'The growth of radicalism made the chance of settlement with the King less likely, 1646–49.' Assess the validity of this view.
3. 'Charles's decision to launch a second civil war was the main reason settlement was not reached by 1649.' Assess the validity of this view.
4. With reference to these extracts and your understanding of the historical context, assess the value of these three sources to an historian studying why settlement was not reached in the years 1646–49.

## Extract A

An extract from the Leveller pamphlet, *The Case of the Army Truly Stated*, 1648   *to army Cncal   oct. → Putny Debats*

The grievances, dissatisfactions and desires of the army, both as commoners and soldiers, have been many months since represented to the Parliament, and the army has waited with much patience to see their common grievances redressed and the rights and freedoms of the nation cleared and secured; … We propound [that] … all power is originally and essentially in the whole body of the people of this nation, and whereas their free choice or consent by their representers is the only original or foundation of all just government … [The] power of the Commons in Parliament is the thing against which the king has contended, and the people have defended with their lives, and therefore ought now to be demanded as the price of their blood … And so this army that God has clothed with honour in subduing the common enemy, may yet be more honourable in the people's eye, when they shall be called the repairers of their breaches, and the restorers of their peace, right and freedom.[15]

## Extract B

An account of the Windsor prayer meeting of May 1648, where officers and agitators of the army met in prayer before fighting the Second Civil War. This account was written by an agitator, William Allen, who published his memoirs in 1659.

[The Lord] did direct our steps, and presently we were led, and helped to a clear agreement amongst ourselves, not any dissenting, that it was the duty of our day, with the forces we had, to go out and fight against those potent enemies, which that year in all places appeared against us … [It was] then debated amongst us, that it was our duty, if ever the Lord brought us back again in peace, to call Charles Stuart, that man of blood, to an account, for that blood he had shed, and these mischiefs he had done, to his utmost, against the Lord's cause and people in these poor nations.[16]

## Extract C

The charge made against the King during his trial, 1649

That the said Charles Stuart, … out of a wicked design to erect and uphold in himself an unlimited and tyrannical power to rule according to his will, and to overthrow the rights and liberties of the people … [and] hath been, and is the occasioner, author, and continuer of the said unnatural, cruel and bloody wars; and therein guilty of all the treasons, murders, rapines, burnings, spoils, desolations, damages and mischiefs to this nation, acted and committed in the said wars, or occasioned thereby.[17]

## Chapter summary

This chapter should have helped you gain an understanding of the failure to reach settlement in the period following the First Civil War. Besides an awareness of the emergence of the army as a political force, you should also understand:

* the reasons why the army and Parliament became political opponents
* the nature of radical groups
* the causes and consequences of Charles I's decision to launch the Second Civil War
* the process by which the trial and execution of the King became possible.

## End notes

1   Coward B. *The Stuart Age: England 1603–1714*. London: Longman; 1994. p. 228.

2   Robertson G. *The Levellers: The Putney Debates*. London: Verso; 2007. p. xviii.

3   Ibid. p. 31–41.

4   Worden B. *The English Civil Wars, 1640–1660*. p. 108–9.

5   Morrill B, Manning D, Underdown D. What was the English Revolution? In Gaunt P. (ed.) *The English Civil War*. p. 25–26.

6   Quoted in Smith DL. *A History of the Modern British Isles, 1603–1707*. Oxford: Blackwell; 1998. p. 172.

7   Quoted in Smith DL. *A History of the Modern British Isles, 1603–1707*. p. 173.

8   Quoted in Smith DL. *A History of the Modern British Isles, 1603–1707*. p. 154.

9   Extracts from the Putney debates can be found in Robertson G. *The Levellers: The Putney Debates*. London: Verso; 2007. This extract is from p. 69.

10   http://bcw-project.org/church-and-state/second-civil-war/putney-debates

11   Purkiss D. *The English Civil War*. London: Harper Perennial; 2007. p. 532–42.

12   Smith DL. *A History of the Modern British Isles, 1603–1707*. p. 161.

13   Wedgwood CV. *The Trial of Charles I*. London: Collins; 1964. p. 128.

14   Quoted in Gardiner SR. (ed.), *The Constitutional Documents of the Puritan Revolution 1625–1660*. Oxford: OUP; 1889. p. 282–84.

15   Quoted in Robertson G. *The Levellers: The Putney Debates*. London: Verso; 2007. p. 31–41.

16   Allen W. A faithful Memorial of that Remarkable Meeting of Many Officers of the Army in England, at Windsor Castle, in the Year 1648 (London, 1659), Thomason Tracts, E 979/3: 4–5. Quoted in Lindley K. *The English Civil War and Revolution*. London: Routledge; 1998. p. 167.

17   Quoted in Gardiner SR. (ed.). *The Constitutional Documents of the Puritan Revolution 1625–1660*. p. 282–84.

# 6 Experiments in government and society, 1648–1660

In this section we will examine how the English Revolution transformed England into a republic and the emergence of Cromwell as Lord Protector. The chapter charts the various experiments in government before finally looking at the reasons for the restoration of Charles II and the monarchy in 1660. We will look into:

- The Third Civil War: the attempted Royalist revival; the defeat and exile of Prince Charles.

- Political radicalism: failure of the Levellers and Diggers and the 'Godly Society'; Quakers, Baptists and other radical sects; the Rump Parliament as an experiment in radical republicanism; the Parliament of the Saints.

- Oliver Cromwell and the Protectorate: profile of Oliver Cromwell; Cromwell's personality and approach to government and his refusal of the Crown; the limits of religious toleration; the Major-Generals; the problem of the succession to Cromwell.

- The monarchy restored: political vacuum after the death of Cromwell; negotiations for the return of the monarchy under Charles II; the legacy of the English Revolution by 1660.

# Introduction

In 1649 England found itself without a monarch. The years that followed were characterised by political experimentation and frustration. The army remained a highly political force and the Rump Parliament entirely dependent upon the army for protection and power. Many people were aware that the revolution had been driven by the army and the small number of MPs who had been willing to back it. Support for the new republic was weak. Royalism was far from dead and as the years passed, many would begin to see it as the only means of delivering the nation from ever-deepening chaos. In the midst of this whirlwind of political experimentation arose a man of considerable talent but obscure background: Oliver Cromwell. The limited successes of his rule have been hotly debated but as long as Cromwell, the Lord Protector, lived, so did the republic. Only in the wake of his death was the son of Charles I able to regain his throne.

## Timeline

| | |
|---|---|
| **1649** | **5 February:** Scots proclaim Charles II King<br>**February–March:** publication of John Lilburne's *England's New Chains Discovered*<br>**17 March:** Act abolishing monarchy<br>**19 March:** Act abolishing House of Lords<br>**April:** First Digger community established on St George's Hill, Surrey (driven away in August)<br>**14–15 May:** Leveller mutineers suppressed<br>**19 May:** England declared a Commonwealth<br>**15 August:** Cromwell lands near Dublin<br>**11 September:** massacre at Drogheda<br>**11 October:** massacre at Wexford |
| **1650** | **2 January:** Engagement Act; all adult males to declare loyalty to the Commonwealth<br>**10 May:** death penalty imposed for adultery<br>**June:** Charles agrees to sign Covenants; arrives in Scotland<br>**22 July:** Cromwell invades Scotland<br>**9 August:** Blasphemy Act<br>**3 September:** Cromwell defeats Royalists at Dunbar<br>**27 September:** Toleration Act; compulsory attendance at parish churches abolished |
| **1651** | **1 January:** Charles crowned at Scone<br>**July–August:** Charles leads Scottish army into England<br>**3 September:** Battle of Worcester; Cromwell defeats Charles<br>**9 October:** Navigation Act |
| **1652** | **19 May:** First Anglo-Dutch War begins |
| **1653** | **20 April:** Cromwell dissolves the Rump Parliament<br>**4 July:** Nominated Assembly convenes<br>**12 December:** Nominated Assembly surrenders power to Cromwell<br>**15 December:** Council of Army Officers adopts Instrument of Government<br>**16 December:** Cromwell installed as Lord Protector |

| 1654 | **5 April:** Treaty of Westminster ends Anglo-Dutch War<br>**28 August:** 'Ejectors' established; county commissioners to expel inadequate ministers and schoolmasters<br>**3 September–22 January 1655:** First Protectorate Parliament<br>**November–December:** George Cony fined and and imprisoned for refusing to pay non-parliamentary customs duties<br>**December:** Western Design launched |
|---|---|
| 1655 | **12–16 March:** Penruddock's Rising; abortive Royalist uprising in Wiltshire<br>**April–May:** failure of Western Design<br>**22 August:** first instructions issued to the Major-Generals |
| 1656 | **7 September–26 June 1657:** first session of second Protectorate Parliament<br>**5–17 December:** Parliament debates Nayler's case; it convicts him of 'horrid blasphemy' and sentences him to savage mutilation |
| 1657 | **28 January:** Cromwell abandons the Major-Generals experiment<br>**23 February:** *The Humble Petition and Advice*; Cromwell offered the crown<br>**8 May:** Cromwell declines the crown<br>**25 May:** Cromwell accepts revised version of *The Humble Petition and Advice*; he is to remain Lord Protector<br>**26 June:** Cromwell's second installation as Lord Protector |
| 1658 | **20 January–4 February:** second session of second Protectorate Parliament<br>**14 June:** Battle of the Dunes<br>**3 September:** Death of Oliver Cromwell; Richard Cromwell becomes Lord Protector |
| 1659 | **27 January–22 April:** Third Protectorate Parliament<br>**7 May:** Rump reinstated<br>**24 May:** Rump demands Richard Cromwell's resignation<br>**July–August:** Booth's Rising<br>**13 October:** army dissolves Rump<br>**20 October:** Monck demands return of the Rump<br>**26 October:** Committee of Safety established<br>**Early December:** Monck begins to march south<br>**7 December:** Committee of Safety disperses; over a week with no government at all<br>**26 December:** three regiments reinstate Rump |
| 1660 | **3 February:** Monck's army arrives in London<br>**21 February:** Monck secures readmission of 'purged' MPs<br>**16 March:** Long Parliament calls 'free elections' and dissolves itself<br>**4 April:** Charles II issues the Declaration of Breda<br>**25 April–13 September:** first session of Convention Parliament<br>**8 May:** Convention Parliament declares Charles II to have been King since 30 January 1649<br>**25 May:** Charles II lands at Dover<br>**29 May:** Charles II enters London |

## The Third Civil War

Many moderates saw the trial and execution of Charles I, which had been driven by the army and the Rump Parliament, as radically illegitimate. It had only been possible because most members of the Long Parliament had been purged by the army. It was thus an illegal act that undermined the very basis of England's ancient constitution. The King's execution did not kill Royalism or convince people that republicanism was the best way forward. Rather, it drove Royalist sympathisers underground. The widespread publication of *Eikon Basilike* in the months following the King's execution pays testament to this fact (see Figure 5.3). As the document stated, the King had been a 'political parent' whose duty it had been 'to seek [his people's] peace in the orthodox profession of the Christian religion' and defend the 'ancient laws of the Kingdom'.[1] So widespread was this belief, that the Rump Parliament found it hard to convince people it had the right to rule.

## The attempted Royalist revival

In England, Royalists went to ground, but in Ireland and Scotland the attempted Royalist revival was serious. Charles, Prince of Wales, the King's eldest son, had escaped to Europe in 1646 and was still free. His existence gave many Royalists a rallying point. Ireland, having been in rebellion since 1641, once again provided the staging post for a potential invasion of England. In January 1649 Charles I's lieutenant in Ireland, the Earl of Ormonde, negotiated an agreement with Irish Catholics to provide troops for an army with which to invade England. The planned invasion would be given naval support from Prince Rupert's Royalist fleet. The need to deal with this military threat meant that, once again, the Rump was forced to impose wartime taxation. From March 1649 onwards, monthly assessments reached a crippling £90 000. As Cromwell assembled a force with which to deal with the Irish Royalists, General Monck, Parliament's military commander in Ireland successfully split Ormonde's Royalist forces by making a separate armistice with the Irish Catholics commanded by O'Neill.

The Royalist threat, however, was not limited to Ireland. With the Rump now considering Scotland a separate country, in February 1649, the Scots, appalled by the unprecedented execution of the British monarch, declared Charles 'King of Great Britain and Ireland and Scotland'. Unlike his father, Charles willingly made a deal with the Scottish Presbyterians, swearing an oath of loyalty to the Covenant and promising to uphold the Presbyterian system. Such promises brought him the support of Lieutenant-General Leslie's army of 22 000 men. England's fledgling republic, fighting a war on two fronts, looked as if it may be strangled in its infancy.

## The defeat and exile of Prince Charles

The job of safeguarding the new republic fell to Cromwell. In August 1649 Cromwell landed near Dublin with 30 000 men to confront the Irish threat. His troops were **veterans** of the civil wars, who had grown used to victory under Cromwell's command and were contented that he had negotiated settlement of their arrears of pay. What is more, Cromwell had secured agreement from the Rump that his soldiers would be paid throughout the coming campaign. They were also content that they were doing God's work. The racial hatred that Cromwell and his men felt for their Irish foes was marked. Not only were the Irish papists, they were also responsible for the shedding of Protestant blood in the Irish Rebellion of 1641 (see Chapter 2). Cromwell enjoyed a series of victories throughout southern and western Ireland. To Cromwell and his men these victories were providential – proof of God's will.

The Irish campaign is infamous for its ferocity. The treatment of the Irish was brutal and at the towns of Drogheda (September 1649) and Wexford (October 1649) it is estimated that 4600 civilians were massacred by the English troops. Cromwell's calls for the towns to surrender had been rejected; this meant that, strictly speaking, he acted within the rules of 17th-century warfare; however, the bloodletting was exceptional. The memory of these pitiless massacres has remained ingrained in the Irish popular memory ever since. To Cromwell and his men, however, they represented vengeance for Protestantism.

On 22 July 1650 Cromwell turned his attention to Scotland and led an army of 16 000 men across the border, eager to strike at Charles before he had time to organise

### Key term

**veterans:** soldiers who had experience in warfare. In this case, soldiers who had fought in the First and Second Civil Wars.

his army. However, supplies were inadequate and this forced Cromwell's invasion to hug the coastline so they could access supply ships. To make matters worse, the Scottish troops under Lieutenant-General Leslie operated a scorched earth strategy, destroying crops and supplies as they withdrew and so denying the English troops local sustenance. With sickness ravaging the English regiments Cromwell halted his army at Dunbar and Leslie struck, cutting off the English line of retreat. Cromwell's heavily outnumbered troops prepared for defeat – Cromwell himself warned Sir Arthur Hesilrige at Newcastle that a Scottish invasion of England was imminent.

The battle of Dunbar began on 2 September 1650, with Leslie's army occupying a commanding position above the town. Shifting his line forward in order for his cannon to be in range, Leslie began a bombardment. However, Leslie had unwittingly left a gap between the flank of his army and the coastline, a weakness that Cromwell exploited. That night Cromwell manoeuvred troops into the gap on Leslie's flank and then launched a dawn assault. The effect was tremendous; by the end of the day Leslie's army was routed and Cromwell had achieved the finest tactical victory of his military career.

For Cromwell this victory was another providential act of God. In his official report to Parliament he compared it to the Biblical story of Gideon's miraculous victory over the Midianites, who far outnumbered the people of Israel. At the same time he implored MPs to pursue a godly reformation and make England worthy of God's blessings; thus he invested all his religious hopes in the Rump Parliament.

The victory also served to split Cromwell's Scottish opponents, with a group of influential Presbyterian ministers and more hardline Covenanters believing that it showed God's disapproval of their Royalist allegiance. Nonetheless, many Scots

### ACTIVITY 6.1

Read Cromwell in Voices from the past and then answer the following questions.

1. Why did Cromwell feel he had been granted victory at Dunbar?

2. In light of this victory, what did Cromwell urge Parliament to do?

## Voices from the past

### *Oliver Cromwell*

**Cromwell's report to Parliament after the taking of Wexford, October 1649**

And indeed it hath not without cause been deeply set upon our hearts, that we intended better to this place than so great a ruin, … yet God would not have it so; but, by an unexpected providence, in his righteous justice, brought a just judgement upon them, causing them to become a prey to the soldier, who in their piracies had made preys of so many families, and made with their blood to answer the cruelties which they had exercised upon the lives of divers poor Protestants.[2]

## Voices from the past

### *Oliver Cromwell*

**Cromwell's official report to the Rump Parliament following his victory at Dunbar, 4 September 1650**

Thus you have the prospect of one of the most signal mercies God hath done for England and His people, this War: … It is easy to say, The Lord hath done this. It would do you good to see and hear our poor foot [soldiers] go up and down making their boast of God. But, Sir, it's in your hands, and by these eminent mercies God puts it more into your hands. To give glory to Him … We that serve you beg of you not to own us, but God alone. We pray you own His people more and more; for they are the chariots and horsemen of Israel. Disown yourselves, but own your authority; and improve it to curb the proud and the insolent … Relieve the oppressed, hear the groans of poor prisoners in England. Be pleased to reform the abuses of all professions; and if there be any one that makes many poor to make a few rich, that suits not a Commonwealth.[3]

remained loyal to their king, and with Cromwell declining to venture any further north than Perth, in January 1651 Charles was crowned at Scone. Swearing to uphold the Covenant as King of Great Britain and Ireland, Charles also vowed to uphold the Covenant to establish Presbyterianism as the religion of all his realms. During the summer Cromwell lured Charles into an ill-judged invasion of England with an army of 13 000 men, but support in England was lacklustre and brought him only a further 2000 recruits. On 3 September 1651, exactly a year after his victory at Dunbar, Cromwell's forces intercepted Charles at Worcester and inflicted a crushing defeat on Charles at Worcester. The battle brought an end to what is referred to as the Third Civil War and Charles fled south, allegedly hiding in an oak tree before crossing the English Channel to exile in France.

# Political radicalism

## Failure of the Levellers and Diggers and the 'Godly Society'

Against the backdrop of the regicide, many radical sects believed that the time had come for a fundamental reorganisation of society. One such group was known as the Diggers, or 'True Levellers', and was led by a failed London shopkeeper called Gerrard Winstanley. The Diggers were early communists who advocated common ownership of property and land. Taking control of waste or common land, the Diggers established small communities across England. The most famous was the first Digger community established on common land on St George's Hill, Surrey, in April 1649. This commune reveals the basis of what their proposed 'Godly Society' would have looked like. At its heart was the belief that before the Norman Conquest in 1066 there had been a golden age in which the rights of English people had been respected and where the Earth was 'a common treasury of all mankind'. The Norman Conquest, they argued, had created a social order that restricted the rights of the people and robbed them of their property and land. Communes like St George's Hill were the first step in building a new 'Godly Society' in which the ancient rights of the people would be revived. The commune lasted four months before it was forcibly broken up by local landowners. Winstanley's last political action was to publish a pamphlet titled *The Law of Freedom* in 1652, which once again argued for a Christian-based society in which all land was to be distributed evenly. After this point the communities soon collapsed and many Diggers found a home in another religious sect, the Quakers.

The unwillingness of the **landed gentry** to accept such radical social change was shown in the new regime's handling of the Levellers. The Levellers' hopes that the *Agreement of the People* would form the basis of a new constitution (see the section on The Rump Parliament as an experiment in radical republicanism) were dashed. The Council of Officers of the Army considered and dismissed the document during the Whitehall debates of December 1648 to January 1649 and the Rump failed to dissolve itself in favour of fresh elections. Convinced that the old order was maintaining its grip on power the leading Levellers unleashed scathing pamphlets at the Rump and the new Council of State, which exercised the powers of head of state (Cromwell was among its 40 members). Lilburne led the way in February and March 1649 with a two-part pamphlet titled *England's New Chains Discovered*. Cromwell's acceptance of the new regime was then damned by Overton's accusation that he had put selfish ambition above the good of the nation, a criticism that he published in his pamphlet *The Hunting of the Foxes*.

Desperate to create a 'Godly Society', the Levellers began to encourage mutiny in the army. Throughout the spring of 1649 Leveller-inspired mutinies erupted among the troops and were supressed by Cromwell and Fairfax. In May 1649 a small band of mutineers was pursued from Salisbury to Burford where it was easily defeated by troops loyal to Cromwell; three of the ringleaders were executed by firing squad. Lilburne, as a civilian, was tried and acquitted but the Leveller movement began

## Key term

**landed gentry:** gentlemen who owned property in the form of land. In order to vote and be part of the political nation, gentlemen had to own large amounts of land.

to drift into obscurity. Any chance of motivating the rank and file of the army into a more serious overthrow of the grandees was thwarted by the Rump's decision to offer soldiers debentures – the right to buy land formally owned by the crown. The dream of building a new, levelled 'Godly Society' was over.

## Quakers, Baptists and other radical sects

The Quakers were well known for their radical religious and social views. Their beliefs centred around the conviction that all individual human beings had within themselves a manifestation of Christ's spirit – an 'inner light'. This belief led them to reject Calvinist and puritanical beliefs that God had predetermined an 'elect' number of people to rise to heaven and that all others were damned to hell. The concept of an 'inner light' also led Quakers to shun all ideas of social hierarchy and superiority, for Christ resided in everyone, rich and poor alike; indeed, it is easy to see why many Levellers were also Quakers. They refused to swear oaths, to pay tithes to the Church, or to doff their hats to anyone of superior social rank. Other Levellers found a religious home among the Baptists who believed, like the Quakers, that no human being was damned to hell. Unlike the Anglican Church, the Baptists did not believe in infant baptism, which was thought to save a child from hell, but believed that people could be saved for Christ through adult baptism (see Table 5.1).

Although socially subversive, the Quakers were not a political body and so were much harder to eliminate than the Levellers. The Ranters, who we have already seen took the idea of 'inner light' to greater lengths (see the section on Ranters and other populist groups in Chapter 5) bore the brunt of persecution, with the Rump passing acts against adultery (May 1650) and blasphemy (August 1650) in an attempt to suppress them. The Quakers, however, quietly continued to multiply throughout the 1650s, and it is thought they numbered around 40 000 by the end of the decade. The presence of such radical sects shaped people's opinions in this period, convincing them that the experiment in republicanism had given rise to social and religious disorder. When the monarchy was finally restored in the 1660s, this mood came to fruition in the Clarendon Codes, a series of laws that ended any sense of religious toleration and defined radical groups like the Quakers and Baptists as non-conformist outcasts.

## The Rump Parliament as an experiment in radical republicanism

The men behind the regicide had been driven by their belief in Charles I's 'blood-guilt' and their religious conviction that God's providence had witnessed against him. What was lacking, however, was a clear political vision of what would follow the execution of the King. Despite the claims made by the Levellers, the regicide did not constitute a bid for power on the part of Cromwell. With the army behind him and the Rump still reeling from Pride's Purge, Cromwell could have easily established himself as head of a new government but he did not. Instead, he submitted himself to the rule of the Rump.

Instead, the Rump simply evolved a new format for government. It took the Rump nearly two months to pass acts abolishing monarchy and the House of Lords. Finally, on 19 May 1649, nearly four months after the King's execution, England was declared a 'Commonwealth and Free State' with supreme authority vested in Parliament. The new sovereignty of Parliament was reinforced in January 1650 by the Engagement – an oath – to be taken by all adult males, swearing that they would be 'true and faithful to the Commonwealth of England, as it is now established, without a King or House of Lords'.[4]

The decision to insist on the Engagement revealed the Rump's insecurity and desperation to legitimise itself. It was also problematic: people were concerned that by swearing loyalty to the regime they were, by inference, declaring their acceptance of the regicide as a legal act. This was too much for lukewarm republicans, many

## ACTIVITY 6.2

Why were Quakers, Baptists and radical sects seen as a danger to social order?

of whom had never intended to see the end of monarchy. It is telling that of the 41 members of the Council of State, only 19 took the Engagement.[5]

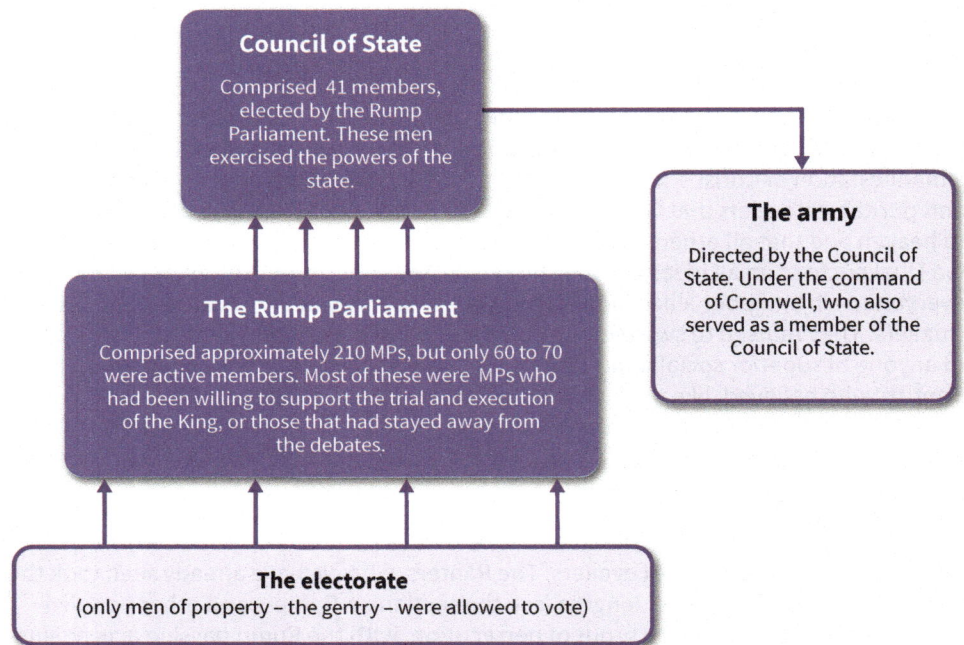

**Council of State**

Comprised 41 members, elected by the Rump Parliament. These men exercised the powers of the state.

**The army**

Directed by the Council of State. Under the command of Cromwell, who also served as a member of the Council of State.

**The Rump Parliament**

Comprised approximately 210 MPs, but only 60 to 70 were active members. Most of these were MPs who had been willing to support the trial and execution of the King, or those that had stayed away from the debates.

**The electorate**
(only men of property – the gentry – were allowed to vote)

**Figure 6.1:** The system of government under the Rump, 1649–53.

Cromwell's euphoria over the victory at Dunbar in 1650 had revealed his fundamental belief that the English were God's chosen people – they were, in Cromwell's mind, the new Israelites of the Bible and England was the Promised Land. A year later, in September 1651, Cromwell had written again to his political masters at Westminster following his second victory over the Scots at Worcester, or the 'crowning mercy' as he called it. In a mood shared by Fifth Monarchists within the army, he urged MPs to pursue an agenda of godly reformation. However, in the months that followed, Cromwell and those who shared his religious zeal were hugely disappointed by the Rump's governance.

The most pressing issue for the Rump was security of the new republic, hence the dispatch of Cromwell and the army to Ireland and Scotland in 1649–51. Of the legislation passed by the Rump, security and finance accounted for a massive 51%, while local government and the army accounted for another 30%. In comparison, religious and legal reforms each accounted for only 3% of legislation.[6] The quality of this legislation was also dubious; the experiment in Presbyterian government of the Church of England introduced in 1646–48 was not repealed, whereas the severe penalties put in place for blasphemy and adultery, fornication and incest saw only four women hanged. Although shocking to the modern mind, this statistic highlights that the laws were not strictly enforced. Although the Rump did bring about modernisation of the legal system, translating all legal proceedings from Latin into English and court hand into ordinary handwriting, other key areas went unchanged. For example, the Hale Commission on law reform proposed radical legal innovation but not one of their proposals was passed into law by the Rump. In short, the Rump MPs were happy to do enough to secure their position but no more. This self-serving attitude was revealed most clearly in the MPs' attitude to **tithes**. Uniformly resented by the lower orders of society, the Rump, happy to serve the interests of the rich and privileged, did nothing to abolish them.

The new Council of Trade, established by the Rump in August 1650 shows they were not entirely self-interested. This was hugely beneficial to the merchant classes and in October 1651 it ensured the passage of the Navigation Act. This Act decreed that English shipping would have the exclusive right to transport goods to and from England and foreign shipping (notably the Dutch) would be forced out of the market. Yet in spite of this success, it was clear that the Rump was becoming more inactive. Out of more than 200 MPs the average attendance dropped to between 50 and 60, and the number of acts passed by the Rump declined progressively from 125 in 1649 to a mere 44 in 1652.

The lethargy of the civilian Rump MPs was not lost on Cromwell and the army leaders. Despite seeking assurances that the Rump would dissolve itself in favour of fresh elections no later than 1654, it was apparent that the Rump was dragging its feet. After returning victorious from Ireland and Scotland, Cromwell met leading MPs and army officers to discuss a bill for a 'new representative'. The proposal was that the Rump would dissolve itself and that elections would be held under the scrutiny of a council of MPs and army officers. Only vetted candidates of zealously religious outlook would be allowed to become MPs. Having made this agreement on 19 April 1653, the very next day Cromwell was alarmed to hear that the Rump was discussing the possibility of dissolving itself in favour of free elections, outside of army influence. Worried that free elections might see the return of Presbyterian MPs who were hostile to the idea of religious toleration and godly reformation, Cromwell rushed from his bedchamber to Parliament allegedly still wearing bed socks under his boots. In a dramatic moment reminiscent of Charles I's entry into Parliament in 1642, Cromwell berated MPs as 'Whoremasters and Drunkards'. 'You have sat here too long for the good you have been doing,' he told them. 'Depart, I say, and let us have done with you. In the name of God, go.' With a wave of his hand he called in troops commanded by the Fifth Monarchist Major-General Thomas Harrison and had the chamber forcibly emptied of MPs. Pointing at the mace – the symbol of Parliament's sovereignty – Cromwell is reported to have uttered in contempt, 'Do away with this bauble.' The soldiers having locked the chamber behind them, some unknown person fixed to the doors a scrap of paper that read, 'This House is to Let'. Power now lay in the hands of Cromwell and the army.

## ACTIVITY 6.3

Read the section on The Rump Parliament as an experiment in radical republicanism.

1. Complete a list of things achieved by the Rump in the period 1649–53. How many of these achievements were in the interests of the gentry rather than the common people?

2. Are we right to see the Rump as an ineffective form of government?

## 🔑 Key term

**tithes:** a tax that was raised to pay for the maintenance of the clergy. However, by the time of the Civil War the right to gather this tax was often held by the gentry, who had purchased the right as a long-term financial investment.

**Figure 6.2:** Cromwell's dismissal of the Rump Parliament in 1653.

> ## Key term
>
> **Sanhedrin:** a council of godly men used to rule in ancient Israel. Fifth Monarchists believed that England should adopt such a holy council as a form of government following the dismissal of the Rump Parliament in 1653.

**Figure 6.3:** 'The Picture of the Good-Old Cause drawn to life': a Royalist pamphlet depicting Praise-God Barebone, one of the more radical Fifth Monarchists who sat in the Nominated Assembly who lent his name to the nickname coined by Royalist commentators, 'Barebone's Parliament'. The nickname ignores the fact that many members of the Assembly were moderate or conservative in outlook. The use of the name was an attempt to discredit the Assembly as a radical horde.

## The Parliament of the Saints

With the Rump dismissed by force, power now lay in the hands of Cromwell and the army. Despite claims that he intended to establish a military dictatorship, it is probably fair to say that this had not been Cromwell's intention. Indeed, Cromwell and his officers spent some considerable time in discussion with civilian ex-Rumpers about the drawing up of 'some instrument of government that might put the power out of his [Cromwell's] hands'.[7] In reality the dismissal of the Rump had been a reactive measure intended to stop an ineffective government that had failed to bring about convincing religious reforms. With a vacuum left by the dismissed Rump, Cromwell now had to come up with a blueprint of what would replace it.

On 30 April 1653, Cromwell announced the temporary solution to be a Nominated Assembly. This was something of a compromise. On the one hand, Major-General Thomas Harrison had pushed for 70 men, appointed from the gathered (or separatist) churches, to form an assembly to rule in the interim until Christ's second coming and the start of the 1000-year reign of King Jesus. Such an assembly was inspired by the Bible and was similar to the Jewish Sanhedrin. On the other hand, Major-General John Lambert urged Cromwell to appoint a 12-man committee to rule until a written constitution could be drawn up.

In the event, both men were disappointed but it was Harrison who had come closest to his aim. Cromwell doubled the size of the Sanhedrin advocated by Harrison and appointed 140 'godly men' – hence the nickname given to the Nominated Assembly, 'The Parliament of the Saints'. Although Lambert was disappointed by this apparent submission to the Fifth Monarchists, it is worth keeping in mind that the 140 members were selected for their political reliability as much as their godly ways, and in reality only 14 members were nominated by the gathered or separatist churches. In fact, although it was nicknamed a 'Parliament', this was really only an interim assembly that Cromwell thought he could trust to advance the cause of godly reformation in

England. Cromwell's enthusiasm in this matter was revealed in his opening speech to their first session (see Voices from the past: Oliver Cromwell).

The Nominated Assembly only passed 29 Acts, but some of these were of real significance. Among them were legalisation of **civil marriage** and compulsory registration of births, deaths and marriages. Yet, when it came to religious reform and 'ushering in the things that God has promised', Cromwell's high hopes were sorely dashed. This was largely because four-fifths of its members were from the gentry, 44 had legal training and 119 had served as Justices of the Peace in their local areas. Ranged against this conservative and more moderate element were radical individuals, like Praise-God Barebone, a London leather-seller, preacher and Fifth Monarchist (see Figure 6.3).

This split between the conservative moderates and the radicals prevented the Nominated Assembly lasting longer than it did. Barely six months after being convened the conservative moderates became frightened by the radical suggestions being put forward. Most alarming to those of legal training was the suggestion that the **Court of Chancery** be abolished and the entire Common Law be codified into a pocket-sized digest. Yet more consternation was caused by changes to the process of appointing church ministers and a vote to abolish tithes, which had been passed by only two votes. Troubled by such radicalism, early on the morning of 12 December 1653, the moderates acted. While the radicals were still at a prayer meeting, 80 moderate MPs voted to dissolve the assembly and in so doing 'delivered up unto the Lord General Cromwell the powers which they received from him'.[9] Cromwell once again held the reins of power.

## Oliver Cromwell and the Protectorate

### Profile of Oliver Cromwell

Oliver Cromwell was born into the lower gentry in 1599 in the county town of Huntingdon. His father was the younger son of Sir Henry Cromwell of Hinchingbrooke House on the outskirts of Huntingdon. By the time Cromwell had attended Huntingdon Grammar School and Sidney Sussex College, Cambridge, his uncle and namesake, Sir Oliver Cromwell, was the head of the family. Having failed to advance the political power of the family, Sir Oliver was forced to sell up and move from Huntingdon. Cromwell's father had been one of 10 children and his inheritance relatively small, so the life Cromwell entered was one on the fringes of gentility. When his father died in 1617 Cromwell left Cambridge and returned to Huntingdon to run the family estate. In 1620 he married the daughter of a wealthy London fur merchant, Elizabeth Bourchier, who bore him nine children.

**ACTIVITY 6.4**

Why do you think conservatives and Royalists happily poured scorn on the Nominated Assembly and nicknamed it Barebone's Parliament?

**Key term**

**Court of Chancery:** a legal body that ensured that laws were applied fairly. It had the power to overrule the judgement of other Common Law courts.

---

**Voices from the past**

### *Oliver Cromwell*

Cromwell's speech at the opening of the Nominated Assembly, 4 July 1653. It was nicknamed 'The Parliament of the Saints' or 'Barebone's Parliament' after one of its more religiously radical members.

I confess I never looked to see such a day as this is – it may be nor you either – when Jesus Christ should be so owned as He is, at this day and in this world … I say you are called with a high call. And why should we be afraid to say or think, that this may be the door to usher in the things that God has promised; which hath been prophesied of; which He hath set the hearts of His people to wait for and expect? Indeed I do think something is at the door; we are at the threshold.[8]

In 1628 Cromwell had been elected as one of Huntingdon's two MPs, but within two years he found himself embroiled in town politics. By this point his uncle had sold Hinchingbrooke and without his influence in Huntingdon politics, Cromwell decided to cut his losses and moved his family a few miles to St Ives. This was a financial as well as a personal crisis for Cromwell and during this period he may have slipped from the status of gentleman to that of yeoman farmer, having to get more involved in the day-to-day running of his farmland. In 1636, however, Cromwell's fortunes were transformed with the inheritance of land near Ely. He moved his family to the city and once again enjoyed the status of a landed gentleman. In 1640, his status was confirmed by his election as MP for Cambridge.

At some point around the time of his move to St Ives, Cromwell appears to have experienced a period of intense depression and soul-searching that amounted to a religious revelation. In a letter written in 1638 he recalled his conversion experience to his cousin, the wife of the Puritan MP Oliver St John. He recalled how God 'giveth springs in a dry and barren wilderness where no water is… the Lord forsaketh me not [and]… if here I may honour my God either by doing or by suffering, I shall be most glad.'[10] This experience shaped Cromwell's outlook on life, confirmed his belief in **Providence** and led him to look for God's will revealed in worldly affairs.

> ### Key term
>
> **Providence:** God's intervention in the world and the lives of people on Earth.

## Cromwell's personality and approach to government and his refusal of the crown

### Cromwell's religious views

The religious revelation Cromwell experienced in his early thirties meant that by the time of the Civil Wars he was a truly devout individual who felt that he had been saved by the Lord. Beyond this image of Cromwell as a godly man, historians have struggled to pin down his personality and personal beliefs with any degree of certainty. Conjecture has arisen from the gaps in the historical record where letters and speeches have been lost; our view has been blurred by the fact that Cromwell was something of a political chameleon, often influenced by the political outlook of those around him. Above all, the longer he lived, the more enemies Cromwell made, and this has left a trail of critical interpretations of Cromwell's actions and motives. For these reasons, it is sometimes hard to reach an objective view on Cromwell – was he an ambitious man, bent on achieving authoritarian government by whatever means necessary? Or, as Cromwell himself would have us believe, was he the reluctant leader called by God to lead his nation when he would rather 'have been living under a woodside to have kept a flock of sheep, rather than to have undertaken such a place as this was'?[11]

Cromwell believed that England and its people had been chosen by God to lead a godly reformation and that he had been saved to play a key role in it. Cromwell's own religious affiliation remains elusive. At birth in 1599 he had been christened in a Protestant Church of England church, but he did not lead a particularly godly lifestyle when resident in Huntingdon: 'I lived in and loved darkness, and hated the light.' His religious revelation in the early 1630s saw him develop a belief that England and its people had the ability to be saved and while he certainly shared some sympathy with Puritan religious discipline, love of the scriptures and lay-preaching, he probably did not believe that there was a predestined elect and that all others were damned to hell. In Cromwell's mind salvation was something that could be found by everyone. This salvation was not something that would be aided by a highly centralised state Church with orders of service, set prayers, ceremony and a bureaucratic system of bishops. Cromwell believed in a more organic godliness – that if people were set free to worship as they saw fit, they would find God. Any church system therefore needed to pay heed to 'tender consciences' and tolerate a range of Protestant denominations. The greatest enemies to God's mission in England were, in Cromwell's mind, the forces of Catholicism and the explosion of blasphemies, religious sects and extremists. As his treatment of the Irish in 1649 proved, his religious toleration only went so far.

## Cromwell's social and political views

From a social and political perspective, Cromwell was much less liberal and remained true to his roots as a member of the gentry. At the Putney Debates in 1647, Cromwell had defended the social and political status quo against radical upheaval. From a settled society, he reasoned, a godly society could grow. He favoured natural hierarchies and found nothing in the scriptures to contradict their usefulness in governing a nation. That said, he was not committed to any particular form of government, and as this chapter explores, he would test a variety of different forms of government throughout the 1650s. His guiding principle was that whatever social and political system best guaranteed the fulfilment of God's 'cause' was acceptable to him. In 1654 he declared to MPs of the first Protectorate Parliament that he had 'four fundamentals' to which any government had to conform. They were government exercised by one man (a head of state) and a parliament; the summoning of regular parliaments that must not be allowed to perpetuate themselves; liberty of conscience in religious affairs; and combined control of the armed forces by the head of state and Parliament.

## Cromwell's 'ideological schizophrenia'

In essence, there were two sides to Cromwell. On the one hand he was a religious radical eager to bring about a godly reformation that would banish the last vestiges of popery; and on the other, he was a social and political conservative eager to settle the nation's wounds and bring about a return to familiar forms of government.

The problem was that many of Cromwell's contemporaries saw these outlooks as contradictory. For centuries, the hierarchies and common messages extolled by the established Church had reinforced and upheld the social and political hierarchy. Weekly sermons reinforced the need to respect one's superiors. In the wake of the Civil Wars people feared that erosion of the Church of England in favour of independence of worship and liberty of conscience would further erode social order. Cromwell, however, saw no such problem. He believed that settlement and religious reform could both be achieved: in April 1657 he told representatives of the second Protectorate Parliament, 'He sings sweetly that sings a song of reconciliation betwixt these two interests.'[12] In reality, his dual outlook and aims were probably mutually exclusive and ensured he made allies and enemies in equal measure, no matter which agenda he followed. Many historians, like Blair Worden, agree that Cromwell suffered from 'ideological schizophrenia'.

## The Instrument of Government

In December 1653 Cromwell found himself in a position of supreme power. The Nominated Assembly had increasingly begun to threaten to end the taxes that supported the army, and this had prompted Major-General Lambert to draft a paper constitution to establish a parliamentary form of government with a single head of state at the fore. This document was called the Instrument of Government – Britain's first written constitution – and became the basis upon which the new political system was established: the Protectorate. This Protectorate, it was hoped, would provide the social and political stability needed to allow godly reform.

When Cromwell rejected the idea of being crowned king, the Instrument of Government gave him the title 'Lord Protector' for life, and thereafter decreed that his successors would be elected by the Council of State that would help him rule. This Council was made up of between 13 and 21 men, elected by a single chamber Parliament. In some ways this three-part system – Protector, Council and Parliament – had echoes of monarchy about it, but it was certainly a limited monarchy. Many of the constraints put on the Lord Protector went back to the demands made on the King in the *Heads of the Proposals* in 1647. The Instrument guaranteed triennial parliaments and decreed that they should sit for a minimum of five months. Laws would be passed by Parliament and Protector, unless in a state of emergency, and until the

**ACTIVITY 6.5**

Look forward to the section on The problem of the succession to Cromwell. Why do you think Cromwell was so reluctant to take the crown both in 1653 and 1657?

first parliament met, during which time Cromwell was permitted to pass ordinances alone. Unsurprisingly for an army document, the Instrument also guaranteed income to support a standing army of 30 000 men, as well as £200 000 a year to maintain civil government. Cromwell's and the army's desire to pursue a godly reformation was reflected in the Instrument, which allowed for members of the Council to exclude MPs who were not of 'known integrity, fearing God'. On a national level a state Church would be maintained that would encourage the 'public profession' of 'sound doctrine'. However, this was not to be compulsory and religious toleration was to be extended to those of 'tender consciences' who 'profess faith in God and Jesus Christ'. This toleration excluded Catholics and the radical sects that injured the moral well-being of the nation.[13]

In this document we can discern the heart of Cromwell's ambitions. Using the support he enjoyed from the military, the Instrument of Government created what was essentially a civilian government. The Protector, constrained by the articles of the Instrument, could not rule as an absolute monarch and his power was not **hereditary**. Rather, Lambert's constitution provided social and political order, with the vote tightly restricted to the landed gentry. This stability, it was hoped, would allow for the continuation of the Reformation that had begun under the Tudors, and which generations of godly men and women had fought to continue in the century that had followed. Now the godly, with Cromwell at their head, wished to bring about a 'reformation of manners' that would make England worthy of the trust Cromwell believed God had placed in the English people, and would mean they would have to 'purify their lives of drunkenness, swearing, adultery, fornication and all other sins'.[14]

Cromwell's optimism was demonstrated in his enthusiastic activity in the months leading up to the opening of the first Protectorate Parliament in September 1654. He and his Council eagerly prepared 82 ordnances in the first nine months of the Protectorate and expected the new MPs to duly ratify these as acts that 'healed and settled' the nation and advanced the godly cause. His speech to the newly assembled Parliament was reflective of his great hopes (see Voices from the past).

## The limits of religious toleration

For all his hopes, Cromwell was soon disappointed. In the first days of the first Protectorate Parliament, the new MPs, many of them Presbyterian gentry or lawyers, demanded the suppression of non-conformist sects and launched a scathing attack on the Instrument of Government – the very constitution that had brought them into being. For some it failed to give enough power to Parliament as it effectively gave Cromwell a veto over legislation and the right to dissolve Parliament once it had been sitting for five months. For those with long memories, this was an erosion of the rights gained in the Own Consent Act of 1641. Others complained that it offended their republican sympathies. Although Cromwell had rejected the title of king, they saw in

---

### Key term

**Hereditary:** Conferred by or based on inheritance.

---

### Voices from the past

#### *Oliver Cromwell*

**Cromwell's address at the Opening of the First Protectorate Parliament, 4 September 1654**

You are met here on the greatest occasion that, I believe, England ever saw, having upon your shoulders the interest of three great nations … And truly, I believe

I may say it without any hyperbole [exaggeration], you have upon your shoulders the interest of all the Christian people in the world … It hath been very well hinted to you this day, that you come hither to settle the interests before mentioned … After so many changes and turnings which this nation hath laboured under, to have such a day of hope as this, and such a door of hope opened by God to us.[15]

his style and title as 'His Highness, the Lord Protector' a worrying echo of monarchy. Indeed, for some critics of Cromwell, his acceptance of the Instrument of Government was proof of his unbridled ambition. On 12 September Cromwell gave a long speech to the unruly MPs, defending the Instrument and outlining the 'four fundamentals' that he believed should underpin any government (see the section on Cromwell's personality and approach to government). In an attempt to bring the MPs into line, Cromwell insisted that they swear a Recognition, pledging loyalty to the Lord Protector and his 'four fundamentals'. For many, including the republican Sir Arthur Hesilrige, this was too much to stomach and about 100 MPs immediately withdrew from Parliament in protest.

Sir Arthur Hesilrige (1601–61) had originally been elected to serve in the Long Parliament of 1640 and was one of the five MPs that Charles I had attempted to arrest in 1642. He fought for Parliament in the First Civil War and remained an active politician in the years that followed. He was a fervent opponent of Cromwell, who he believed was abusing his military power. After Cromwell's death in 1658 Hesilrige continued to challenge military-dominated forms of government and was a strong critic of General John Lambert.

The departure of Hesilrige and the critical MPs did little to improve the productivity of the Parliament or build on the ordinances Cromwell had prepared, including the union with Scotland and the treaty that ended the first Dutch War that had started in 1652. Most frustrating was Parliament's refusal to continue the programme of religious reform. A number of Cromwell's ordinances had encouraged religious discipline, for example the establishment of a national body that would examine all new clergy before allowing them to preach. He also prepared the ground for the appointment of 'ejectors' who in August 1654 were sent into the counties to expel ministers and schoolmasters. Instead, the remaining MPs began to redraft the Instrument line by line, and then in a final affront to Cromwell's wishes they launched assaults on the provision for liberty of conscience and freedom of worship. This was the last straw and at the earliest possible opportunity Cromwell invoked his right to dissolve Parliament after only five months – so eager was Cromwell to put an end to their sitting that he actually counted in lunar, rather than calendar, months. On 22 January 1655 Cromwell reprimanded the troublesome MPs for 'throwing away precious opportunities' and, fulfilling his 'duty to God and the people of these nations', brought their sitting to an end.

## The Major-Generals

In the months following the dissolution of the first Protectorate Parliament, Cromwell's rule aroused much criticism, not least because it resembled the Personal Rule of Charles I. Cromwell believed that at times it was necessary that the people be ruled 'for their good, not what pleases them'. In a blatant disregard for the law he willingly imprisoned people without trial on the grounds that they threatened the peace of the land, and in November 1654 he imprisoned a London silk merchant named George Cony for refusing to pay customs duties that had not been approved by Parliament. Such actions only sharpened the accusations of high-handed ambition.

Particularly worrying for Cromwell, however, was the fact that in March 1655 a Royalist uprising in Wiltshire, led by John Penruddock, revealed the Protectorate's lack of popular support. Although the rising of only a few hundred men was easily crushed by the army (with the assistance of Cromwell's Secretary of State and spymaster-general, John Thurloe), the local population had done nothing to prevent it. His worries were made worse when, in April 1655, news reached Cromwell that his attempt to safeguard English merchants in the Spanish-held Caribbean – the 'Western Design' – had met disaster. Although Jamaica had been captured, the attack on the Spanish island of Hispaniola had been easily repulsed. God, it seemed, was acting against Cromwell and the English, and this providential reading of events threw the Lord Protector into

This map shows the districts commanded by the Major-Generals and their deputies.

● Garrison towns

**Duties**

- Disperse unlawful meetings and gatherings
- Enforce law and order
- Maintain security of the Republic and monitor movement of royalist sympathisers (they were prevented from travelling except with a permit)
- Enforce the Decimation Tax on royalists
- Replace Lords Lieutenant, and manage existing systems of local government

**Actions**

- Raised temporary militia units to help enforce law and order
- Supervised collection of taxation
- Closed alehouses and banned stage plays
- Banned sports like cock-fighting and horse-racing
- Arrested people for drunkenness, sexual licentiousness, swearing and blasphemy

(Howard)

LAMBERT

(Lilburne)

WORSLEY

WHALLEY

BERRY

(Dawkins & Nicholas)

BUTLER

FLEETWOOD

SKIPPON

KELSEY

DESBOROUGH

GOFFE

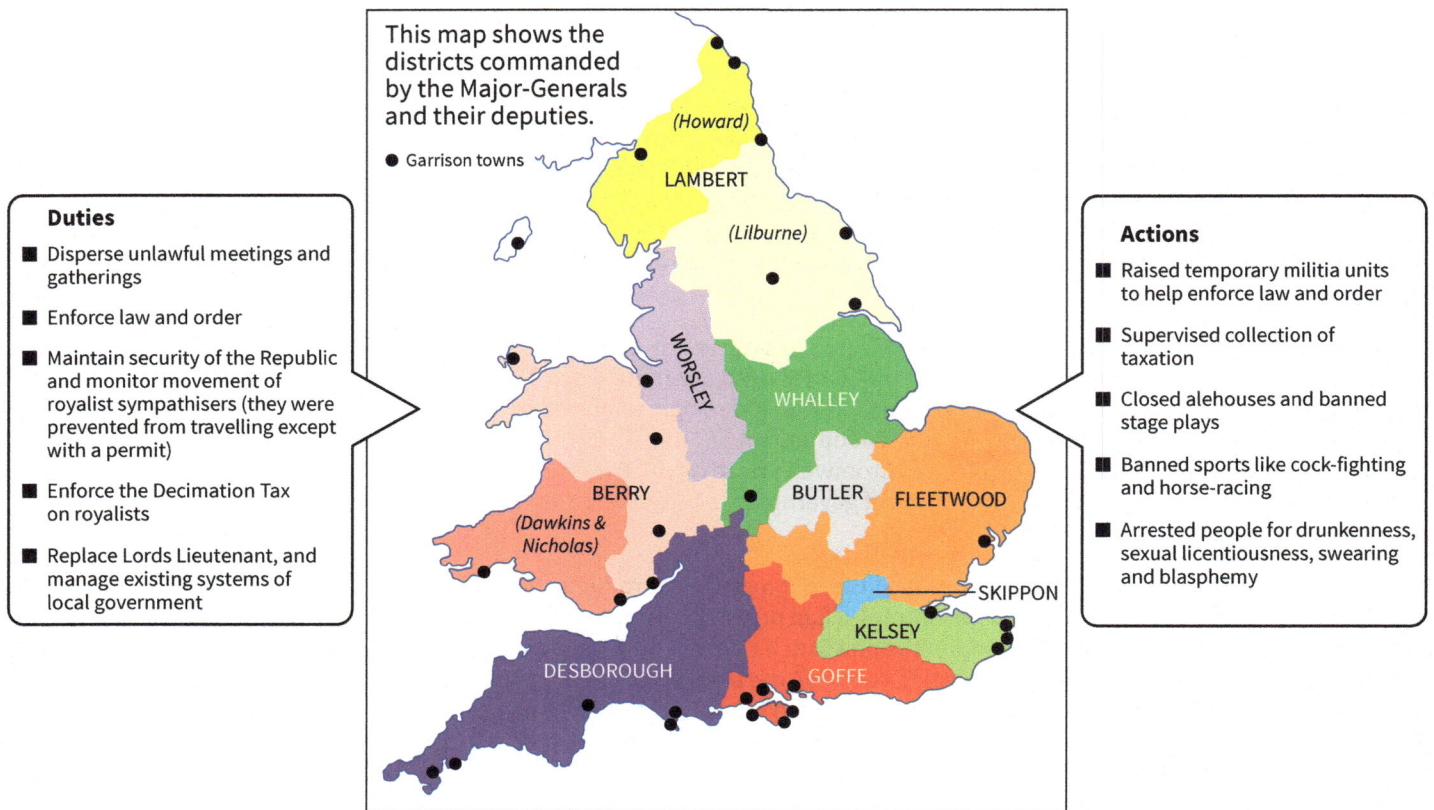

**Figure 6.4:** The Rule of the Major-Generals 1655–57

## ACTIVITY 6.6

1. Create a list of why the Major-Generals caused resentment in the localities.

2. Using your list to help you, what do you think best explains their unpopularity:

   - their religious outlook
   - their attempts to impose law and order
   - the social standing of the officers
   - the cost of maintaining the army
   - their harsh treatment of ex-Royalists

3. Are any of the factors listed here connected?

great distress. Determined to appease God, Cromwell decided that England needed to repent and that using the only reliable support he had – the army – they should advance the 'reformation of manners'.

On 9 August 1655, Cromwell divided England and Wales into 10 (later 11) districts, each to be governed by a Major-General. Their mission was twofold. First, in order to prevent uprisings like Penruddock's, they were to ensure law and order, suppress unlawful assemblies and gatherings, disarm papists and suspected Royalists and quell any sign of threat to the Protectorate. Second, they were to encourage the moral regeneration of the people, challenging all 'profaneness and ungodliness'. Laws against blasphemy and drunkenness were to be enforced and all horse racing, cock fights, bear-baiting and plays were to be stopped. To assist the army the Major-Generals were given permission to establish new regional militias that would be supported by a new 'Decimation Tax'. This tax of 10% of income was levied against all former Royalists. So crippling was it that many were forced to sell their estates in order to pay it.

Although Cromwell felt justified in using military force to advance his dual cause of healing and settling and godly reformation, it was not received well in the regions. The local experience depended entirely on the Major-General in charge, with some vociferously persecuting former Royalists by enforcing the Decimation Tax, while others focused more on suppressing vice and sin. However, the rejection of military rule by local gentry and elites was widespread. These men were used to running local affairs and the imposition of military rule from central government clearly put their noses out of joint. Furthermore, the fact that many of the Major-Generals and their officers had been promoted on merit and had not originated from the gentry (and were thus their social inferiors) was an affront to their dignity. This experiment in military rule led many critics at the time, as well as in the centuries since, to label Cromwell a military dictator. Certainly, there was much about it that was authoritarian and relied on brute force; however, historians more recently have reached consensus over the fact that while Cromwell was certainly willing to fall back on the military as a last resort, his overall commitment to ruling with a parliament means we should not see him as a military dictator.

The rule of the Major-Generals lasted from August 1655 until January 1657, and in the end simply fizzled out. In September 1656, Cromwell had realised that the war against Spain following the failure of the 'Western Design' and a potential extension of hostilities in Flanders required increased revenue. Accordingly he called elections for his second Protectorate Parliament, confident that the presence of the Major-Generals in the regions would ensure the return of godly MPs. Once again, he was disappointed. Such was the hostility towards the Decimation Tax and the excesses of the Major-Generals, the elections were dominated by cries of 'No Swordsmen! No Decimators!' In an attempt to control the MPs Cromwell's Council of State excluded nearly 100 'ungodly' MPs on the first day and still more quit in protest. Yet the remaining MPs maintained their hostility to military rule, defeating Desborough's Militia Bill, which would have secured a renewal of the Decimation Tax. With their funding lost, Cromwell was forced to abandon the rule of the Major-Generals on 28 January 1657.

## The problem of the succession to Cromwell

When the rule of the Major-Generals ended and the second Protectorate Parliament showed itself to be as hostile to the Instrument of Government as the first, Cromwell had only a little over 18 months left to live. In these last months he continued to push forward his godly agenda against his hostile Parliament. He was determined to advance the cause of religious toleration for the full range of Protestant denominations. As early as 1648 he had written to his cousin Robert Hammond that 'I profess to thee I desire it in my heart, I have prayed for it, I have waited for the day to see union and right understanding between the godly people (Scots, English, Jews, Gentiles, Presbyterians, Independents, Anabaptists, and all).'[16] This attitude clearly extended into the last years of his life, for in 1655 Cromwell readmitted the Jews into England (they had been expelled by Edward I in 1290) in the hope that it would secure their conversion to Christianity. In December 1656 Cromwell had also intervened in the James Naylor case. Naylor, a leading Quaker, had re-enacted Christ's entry into Jerusalem on Palm Sunday by riding into Bristol on an ass with women strewing palm leaves in his path. Seeing this as blasphemous behaviour from a socially dangerous sect, Parliament pushed for the death sentence. Cromwell, feeling Parliament had overstepped its constitutional limits, intervened and saved Naylor's life, although the man was still imprisoned, flogged, branded and had his tongue bored through with a red-hot spike. This event highlights how Cromwell's desire for religious toleration (Naylor was one of God's children) brought him into conflict with MPs whose views clearly differed from his.

It was during the second Protectorate Parliament that supporters of Cromwell began to split into two definable groups. On the one hand there was Lambert and others who supported the Instrument, largely military men who advocated godly reform and who have been termed the 'Old' or 'Radical' Cromwellians. Dissenting from this group were the 'New' or 'Conservative' Cromwellians. These were largely civilians who supported Cromwell's leadership but wanted to see the powers of the Protector limited and Parliament's extended. These MPs, including Lord Broghill (a former Royalist in the first Civil War), felt that making Cromwell king was the best way to place constraints on his power. As such, the New Cromwellians drew up a new paper constitution titled, *The Humble Petition and Advice*.

In its first form *The Humble Petition and Advice* offered Cromwell the crown – an offer that threw him into two months of anguish over whether or not to accept. Cromwell had always acknowledged that familiar forms of government would help aid the healing and settling process – the English were familiar with monarchy and it would give the regime legitimacy. However, Cromwell rejected the offer of the crown on the basis that God had witnessed against not only the Stuart monarchy but also the institution of monarchy itself. On 13 April 1657 he told MPs, 'I will not seek to set up that, that providence hath destroyed and laid in the dust; and I would not build **Jericho** again.' On 8 May he finally rejected the crown in favour of a modified version of *The Humble Petition and Advice*, which he accepted as the new constitution on 25 May 1657 (thus replacing the Instrument of Government and forcing Lambert's resignation) and which retained his title as Lord Protector. His decision to reject the crown was certainly motivated by his providential belief, but was also spurred on by the Old Cromwellians and the army more generally. These men, his old supporters, would see his acceptance of the crown as a gross betrayal of the 'good old cause' for which they had fought throughout the Civil Wars. Many officers threatened to resign over the issue and it was the fact that Cromwell still saw the army as 'God's instrument' that persuaded him to decline the offer of kingship.

That said, there was no escaping the kingly nature of his renewed status as Lord Protector, as whom he signed his name in regal style, 'Oliver P', and was addressed as 'Your Highness'. The ceremony that reinstalled Cromwell as Lord Protector in June 1657 bore all the hallmarks of a royal coronation. He wore a purple ermine-lined robe, wore a crown, held a sceptre and swore a modified version of the royal coronation oath. Cromwell hoped that accepting the modified terms of the *The Humble Petition and Advice* would bring more conservative and moderate MPs into line, but in effect it showed the near impossibility of building consensus. On the one hand the Old Cromwellians and army officers were suspicious of the move to make Cromwell a 'king in all but name', whereas the New Cromwellians were disappointed that he had stopped short of taking the full regal title. These tensions continued to simmer below the surface until the very end.

*The Humble Petition and Advice* changed government by rebranding the Council of State a 'Privy Council' of up to 21 members. It also created an 'Other House' as an upper chamber in Parliament. Its members, selected by Cromwell and ratified by the Commons, held no title, but it was in effect a reconstituted House of Lords. Eager to use it as a check to the religiously intolerant attitude of MPs, Cromwell filled it with trusted allies and senior officers from the army. In a further return to 'known ways', Cromwell was granted the right to name his own successor and thus establish a hereditary dynasty if he wished. Provision for a standing army was maintained and a yearly income of £1.3 million was guaranteed from Parliament. With a settlement seemingly reached, in June 1657 the first session of the second Protectorate Parliament went into recess.

When the second session reassembled on 20 January 1658, it did so under the auspices of the new *Humble Petition and Advice* and the hostile MPs excluded in September 1656 were readmitted. With many of Cromwell's supporters promoted to the new upper chamber, the Commons became unruly. Republicans led by Sir Arthur Hesilrige once again attacked the Protectorate's legitimacy, this time focusing on the creation of a House of Lords in all but name. A number of army officers, some from Cromwell's old regiment, began to claim that the Protectorate had abandoned 'the good old cause', forcing Cromwell to have them removed from their commands. Cromwell had little choice but to dissolve Parliament after only two weeks' sitting, on 4 February 1658. The remaining months saw the financial burdens increase and despite the £1.3 million income guaranteed by *The Humble Petition and Advice*, by the end of Cromwell's life there was a national debt of £2.5 million. In foreign policy at least Cromwell must have found satisfaction, with an Anglo-French victory over the Spanish at the battle of the Dunes (14 June) and the defeat of a Spanish assault on Jamaica ten days later. Whatever Cromwell intended to do next is unknown, because in August 1658 he fell ill, probably with a kidney infection. Cromwell died at Whitehall on 3 September 1658, as a great storm howled. It was to prove a pathetic fallacy.

## Key term

**Jericho:** an impregnable walled city mentioned in the Bible. The Book of Joshua records how the Israelites, God's chosen people, were able to capture the city when God chose to strike down the city walls. The destruction of the walls was clearly an expression of God's will.

## ACTIVITY 6.7

Create a list of reasons why Cromwell did the following things:

1.  Rejected the offer of the Crown.
2.  Accepted a modified version of the Humble Petition and Advice.

The title and burden of Lord Protector fell to Cromwell's son, Richard Cromwell. With little or no training as heir, Richard was ill suited to the demands of the situation. He had no military experience and his education had been that of a country gentleman, not a head of state in waiting. In his defence, Richard seems to have been eager to make the civilian-dominated parliamentary system work and was in all things a moderate. From a religious perspective he was probably a Presbyterian and so had some sympathy for the more conservative and moderate MPs. The problem was that the strength of his opponents was altogether too great – he was distrusted by the Old Cromwellian army officers as well as civilian republicans like Hesilrige who wanted to bring about the return of the Rump. Although he received some support from Cromwell's old ally, Major-General George Fleetwood, it is likely that Fleetwood was simply attempting to use Richard as a puppet for the army's interests. Indeed, in the autumn of 1658 Fleetwood tried unsuccessfully to persuade Richard to give up the post of commander-in-chief of the army in favour of himself.

With the national debt of £2.5 million outstripping income by nearly £1 million, Richard was forced to call a third and final Protectorate Parliament, which assembled on 27 January 1659.

Two major issues immediately exploded. Firstly, the republicans, led by Hesilrige, renewed their attack on the Protectorate and argued for a repeal of *The Humble Petition and Advice*. On the other hand the army officers were infuriated by moderate Presbyterian MPs who wanted to restrict the power of the army, placing it once again under Parliament's control. Elements of the army threatened mutiny, and when Major-General Fleetwood informed Richard that he could not guarantee that bloodshed would not follow, Richard gave in and dissolved the third Protectorate Parliament. Two weeks later, on 7 May 1659, the army persuaded Richard that the only option open to him was to recall the Rump Parliament – they hoped that this would help cloak what would otherwise be seen as naked military rule. Alas, when the recalled Rump reassembled on 7 May 1659, it soon became clear that it was not going to be an obedient servant of the army. Instead, it refused to acknowledge the legitimacy of the Protectorate and on 24 May Richard was forced to resign his position as Lord Protector. Richard, perceptive enough to see that he had done all he could, and unable to call upon sufficient loyal troops to contest the situation, gave in and went peacefully. The Cromwellian Protectorate was at an end and the Commonwealth was once again without a head.

## The monarchy restored

### Political vacuum after the death of Cromwell

The failure of Richard left a political vacuum. The army leaders, notably Fleetwood and Lambert, were keen to seize control of affairs, but ranged against them were the republican civilian MPs in the newly recalled Rump, led by Sir Arthur Hesilrige. Both sides were eager to subdue the other but both realised that the other was a 'regrettable necessity', with the Rump lending legitimacy and disguising the army's political power, and the army providing the military force required to safeguard the republic. This was most clearly seen in the eruption of a Presbyterian and pro-Royalist uprising in Cheshire and Lancashire in July 1659, led by Sir George Booth. It is interesting to note that Booth's rising did not directly demand the return of Prince Charles, but instead called for free elections for a fresh Parliament. In reality, this amounted to the same thing, as the growing consensus in the country at large was that the republican experiment had failed and that the best thing now would be to elect a new Parliament that could negotiate a restoration of the monarchy. Alas, the rising was poorly conceived and by August 1659 Lambert had crushed Booth's supporters.

With the immediate Royalist threat suppressed, the Rump attempted to seize the initiative. It declared all acts passed since its forced dissolution in 1653 illegal and

**ACTIVITY 6.8**

Create a timeline showing the end of the republic. It should chart events from Cromwell's death on 3 September 1658 to the arrival of Monck in London on 3 February 1660.

then tried to purge key supporters of the old Protectorate from the army and local government. This was too much for Lambert to stomach and so once again, on 13 October, the Rump MPs found Parliament forcibly dissolved at the point of the sword. In a desperate attempt to screen its political illegitimacy, the army established a Committee of Safety headed by General Fleetwood and his and Lambert's supporters with only a few token civilians.

The cycle of army coups, however, was nearly at an end, for it was at this juncture that the army split. The dissolved Rumpers appealed to General George Monck, commander of the English troops in Scotland, for support, and so found their champion. Monck, himself a former Royalist in the First Civil War, was now utterly disillusioned with the republican experiment and its associated chaos; in his words, he 'dare not sit still and let our laws and liberties go to ruin'.[17] Monck turned his regiments south, determined to take the capital and so secure the reestablishment of the Rump.

George Monck (1608–70) was a professional soldier who had fought in the campaigns against Spain and France in the 1620s as well in the Netherlands in the 1630s. He served in the Royalist army in the First Civil War until he was captured in 1644. Following the King's defeat and subsequent execution Monck joined Cromwell in his Irish and Scottish campaigns. He was instrumental in subduing Scotland but kept a keen eye on affairs in England. It was to Monck that civilians MPs like Hesilrige turned in 1659 to challenge the army's growing dominance in political affairs. Monck would play a pivotal role in the restoration of Charles II in 1660.

The Committee of Safety, faced with Monck's imminent arrival in England, unrest in the fleet, riots in London and a deepening economic depression, was entirely unfit for the job at hand. It hurriedly dispatched General Lambert north to Yorkshire to intercept Monck's advance. Meanwhile, the regiments in London panicked and in a desperate attempt to retain some sort of grip on power actually reinstated the Rump MPs – but it was now too little too late. On 1 January 1660 General Monck crossed the border at Coldstream and began his famous five-week march on London. Brushing Lambert's forces aside in Yorkshire and having covered 350 miles, he arrived in the capital on 3 February 1660, securing the Rump's grip on power.

## Negotiations for the return of the monarchy under Charles II

Monck's intervention was decisive in providing civilian MPs with the military power they had hitherto lacked. At the same time it gave the nation the confidence to air grievances. As Monck moved south from Scotland he received a barrage of petitions expressing people's dissatisfaction with the chaos of republican rule (see Voices from the past: A Petition of the Gentlemen of Devon, 1659). Monck was astute in handling the unravelling situation. Having been in secret communication with the exiled Court he was aware that any restoration of the monarchy needed to emerge from Parliament itself. If not, there was a good chance that there would be a knee-jerk reaction from either republicans or those who had supported the Protectorate and further bloodshed and turmoil could erupt. Thus, Monck moved to secure the Restoration by more subtle means. First, the grateful Rump agreed to Monck's demand that it should readmit the MPs who had been purged by Colonel Pride in 1648, thus turning the Rump back into the Long Parliament. This was significant because it had been these MPs who had been willing to continue negotiations with the King rather than support his trial and execution. This transformation of Parliament then facilitated Monck's second demand that the Long Parliament dissolve itself on 16 March 1660 in favour of free elections. Although the official writs calling the election demanded that former Royalists could not stand as MPs, it was inevitable that the new Parliament, known as the Convention Parliament, had a strong body of MPs who were sympathetic to the Royalist cause, and who were eager to see a Restoration of the monarchy as a means of securing peace, stability and order.

### Voices from the past

## A Petition of the Gentlemen of Devon, 1659

Since the death of the King, we have been governed by tumult; bandied from one faction to the other; this party up today, that tomorrow – but still the nation under, and a prey to, the strongest. So long as this violence continue over us, no other government can settle the nation than that which pleases the universality of it. You speak of the necessity of a republic. We say it is not necessary, not even effectual, but if it were both, a free parliament ought to introduce it. The consent of the people must settle the nation, the public debt must be secured out of the public stock, and interests of opinion and property must be secured by a free parliament.[18]

As the elections for the Convention Parliament unfolded in the spring of 1660, Charles simply had to sit tight and wait. To appeal further to the people of England, Monck in collaboration with Charles's trusted advisors, Edward Hyde and the Earl of Ormonde, urged him first to move from exile in Catholic France to the Protestant Netherlands, and then to issue a Declaration. This was a political masterstroke, for in an instant the Declaration of Breda allayed any fears people might have had about a return to monarchy. In the Declaration Charles promised to work with a 'free Parliament' to settle the nation, to grant a free pardon to all but a few individuals (to be decided in agreement with Parliament), and to settle army arrears of pay and legal contests over land resettlement for Royalists who had lost their estates. In an echo of the policies of the **Interregnum**, he declared that he would grant 'a liberty to tender consciences', and thus allayed any fears that he might wish to impose a Church settlement similar to that of Archbishop Laud in the 1630s. The Convention Parliament, both Commons and Lords, which assembled on 25 April 1660 showed its Royalist sympathies and on 8 May both Houses voted unanimously to offer Charles II the crown on the basis of the Declaration of Breda. At a stroke, Charles was declared to have been the rightful king ever since the moment the executioner's axe had severed his father's head, and all government since was declared illegal. On 25 May, with Edward Montagu having secured the loyalty of the navy, Charles II was carried across the English Channel and landed at Sandwich near Dover. In an act of revealing symbolism, Montagu's ship, *The Naseby*, in which the King was transported, was triumphantly renamed *The Royal Charles*; it was clear to all that Britain was undergoing a moment of transformation. In a grand procession, accompanied by raucous celebration, the King entered London on 29 May 1660. The Royalist diarist John Evelyn recorded: 'I stood in the Strand, and beheld it, and blessed God: and all this without one drop of blood, and by that very army which rebelled against him.'[19]

### Key term

**Interregnum:** literally meaning 'between reigns', this term is used to describe the period between 1649 when Charles I was executed and 1660 when Charles II was restored.

## The legacy of the English Revolution by 1660

The Restoration marked a return to 'normality', but two decades of tumultuous crisis and war, collectively known as 'the English Revolution', would inevitably leave their mark.

Politically, the Restoration saw the three elements of the ancient constitution, Crown, Lords and Commons, reunited into a single body politic. However, as the historian David Smith has commented, 'Although the radical surgery and mutilation that the body politic had suffered during the previous 20 years could be cleverly disguised, they could never be forgotten.'[20] As the Restoration settlement unfolded in the years that followed, many of the issues surrounding the political powers of the Crown and Parliament that had dominated the 'paper combats' of 1640–42 once again raised their heads. In particular, the question of regular parliaments continued as the Triennial

Act was repealed and then reissued in a weaker form. Appointments of ministers and advisors once again reverted to the King and again Parliament was willing to use its control of finances as a political bargaining tool. Despite this, by 1660 the political nation was desirous of compromise between Crown and Parliament. The upheaval and failure to secure a lasting republican system persuaded many that monarchy might not have been the perfect political system, but it was certainly better than the alternatives.

The Revolution also put the importance of economic stability into sharp focus. The need for ample funds for government had proved to be a stumbling block throughout the two decades of upheaval. The willingness of parliaments to use control of the purse strings to advance their interests had often led to political deadlock and worsening relations. The emergence of a standing army complicated matters, and the cost of paying the army remained a constant headache for government. This experience prompted some moves to establish a regular income for the Crown; however, in an echo of the failure of the Great Contract of 1610, Parliament once again seemed reluctant to give up their control of subsidies for fear that it would give the monarch freedom of action. This worry also revealed itself in the unwillingness of MPs to allow the King his old prerogative rights such as Ship Money, feudal dues, and distraint of knighthood. In this sense, the Revolution had changed little, for at the same time MPs still expected that the King should 'live of his own', using private income to fund public duties.

One of the most deeply felt legacies of the Revolution was social. The experience of Cromwell's 'reformation of manners' had been highly unpopular, as it saw the repression of popular cultural pursuits that were deeply entrenched in the social life of local communities. The closure of popular entertainments was seen as draconian and stifling. This ensured that the general population welcomed the culturally liberal nature of the restored monarchy; the excessive and indulgent lifestyle of the restored Royal Court, with all of its newly acquired European tastes, was not necessarily representative of everyday life, but it is true that the restoration of the 'Merry Monarch' certainly indicated a significant cultural shift. Alehouses reopened, dramatic performances and literature thrived, and in time major scientific and academic endeavours were fostered under the auspices of the Royal Society.

Unsurprisingly, it was the religious legacy that was the greatest. Despite Charles's attempt to offer 'liberty for tender consciences' in the Declaration of Breda, it was ironic that it was the Cavalier Parliament, elected in May 1661, that challenged Charles's promise of religious toleration. Clearly stung by the experience of having seen the Church of England eroded, MPs created a strict, compulsive and narrow state Church to which everyone was expected to conform. The Clarendon Codes (a series of laws passed in the wake of the Restoration) punished non-conformist sects and drove them into isolation. They were not destroyed but they became insular and self-sustaining non-conforming communities that would survive for centuries to come. In the more immediate future, the English Revolution ensured that religious affiliation became bound up with political loyalty to the State, with Catholicism remaining the ultimate expression of disloyalty.

In time, many of the political and religious tensions left by the English Revolution would be played out in the Glorious Revolution of 1688. The significant difference, however, was the lack of blood that was shed and in that sense at least, the English Revolution had left an lasting impression upon those who had witnessed the horrors and turmoil of a 'world turned upside down'.

## Further reading

There is a wealth of literature on Cromwell and this period of the English Revolution. A comprehensive overview of the Protectorate can be found in Coward B. *The Cromwellian Protectorate.* Manchester: Manchester University Press; 2002. More detailed insights into Cromwell and aspects of his rule are presented in two excellent collections, first, Smith DL. (ed.). *Cromwell and the Interregnum: The Essential Readings.* Oxford: Blackwell; 2003 and second, Morrill J. (ed.) *Cromwell and the English Revolution.* London: Longman; 1990. For a comprehensive study of the rule of the Major-Generals you can do no better than to consult Durston C. *Cromwell's Major-Generals: Godly Government during the English Revolution.* Manchester: Manchester University Press; 2001. For Christopher Hill's classic Marxist interpretation of Cromwell, see Hill C. *God's Englishman: Oliver Cromwell and the English Revolution.* Longman: Penguin; 1970.

---

### Practice essay questions

1. 'The Rump Parliament failed in 1653 due to its own self-interest and inactivity.' Assess the validity of this view.
2. 'The limited success of the Protectorate can be explained by Cromwell's conflicting aims.' Assess the validity of this view.
3. 'George Monck was the key to the Restoration of the monarchy in 1660.' Assess the validity of this view.
4. With reference to these extracts and your understanding of the historical context, assess the value of these three sources to an historian studying Cromwell's aims.

---

## Extract A

Cromwell's report to Parliament after the taking of Wexford, October 1649

And indeed it hath not without cause been deeply set upon our hearts, that we intended better to this place than so great a ruin, … yet God would not have it so; but, by an unexpected providence, in his righteous justice, brought a just judgement upon them, causing them to become a prey to the soldier, who in their piracies had made preys of so many families, and made with their blood to answer the cruelties which they had exercised upon the lives of divers poor Protestants. [21]

## Extract B

Cromwell's official report to the Rump Parliament following his victory at Dunbar, 4 September 1650.

Thus you have the prospect of one of the most signal mercies God hath done for England and His people, this War: … It is easy to say, The Lord hath done this. It would do you good to see and hear our poor foot [soldiers] go up and down making their boast of God. But, Sir, it's in your hands, and by these eminent mercies God puts it more into your hands. To give glory to Him … We that serve you beg of you not to own us, but God alone. We pray you own His people more and more; for they are the chariots and horsemen of Israel. Disown yourselves, but own your authority; and improve it to curb the proud and the insolent … Relieve the oppressed, hear the groans of poor prisoners in England. Be pleased to reform the abuses of all professions; and if there be any one that makes many poor to make a few rich, that suits not a Commonwealth.'[22]

**Extract C**

Cromwell's address at the Opening of the First Protectorate Parliament, 4 September 1654.

Gentlemen, You are met here on the greatest occasion that, I believe, England ever saw, having upon your shoulders the interest of three great nations, with the territories belonging to them. And truly, I believe I may say it without any hyperbole [exaggeration], you have upon your shoulders the interest of all the Christian people in the world … It hath been very well hinted to you this day, that you come hither to settle the interests before mentioned … After so many changes and turnings which this nation hath laboured under, to have such a day of hope as this, and such a door of hope opened by God to us.' [23]

## Chapter summary

By the end of this chapter you should have gained a broad overview of the Interregnum and the experiments in government that it witnessed. In particular you should understand:

- the reasons for Charles II's failed attempts to regain his throne via campaigns in Ireland and Scotland
- the diversity of radical groups that existed
- the failure of the Rump Parliament to sustain republican forms of government
- the significance of Cromwell's divergent aims in hindering the success of the Protectorate
- the growing problems that Britain experienced during the Protectorate and the period that followed Cromwell's death and how it contributed to the Restoration
- the legacy of the English Revolution by 1660.

## End notes

1   *Eikon Basilike* quoted in Cust R. *Charles I: A Political Life.* London: Pearson; 2007. p. 446.

2   Lomas SC. (ed.). *The Letters and Speeches of Oliver Cromwell, with Elucidations by Thomas Carlyle.* London: Methuen; 1904. Vol. I, p. 486–87.

3   Ibid. p. 108.

4   Quoted in Smith DL. *A History of the Modern British Isles, 1603–1707.* Oxford: Blackwell; 1998. p. 171.

5   Seel GE. *The English Wars and Republic.* London: Routledge; 2005. p. 71–72.

6   Lynch M. *The Interregnum, 1649–60.* London: Hodder; 2002. p. 33.

7   Edmund Ludlow quoted in Coward B. *The Cromwellian Protectorate.* Manchester: Manchester University Press; 2002. p. 10–11.

8   Cromwell quoted in Coward B. *The Cromwellian Protectorate.* p. 10.

9   Smith DL. *A History of the Modern British Isles, 1603–1707.* p. 184.

10  Oliver Cromwell in a letter to his cousin, Elizabeth St John, 1638. Quoted in Gaunt P. *Oliver Cromwell.* New York: NYUP; 2004. p. 37.

11  Roots I. (ed.). *Speeches of Oliver Cromwell.* London: Everyman; 1989. p. 189.

12  Lomas SC. (ed.). *The Letters and Speeches of Oliver Cromwell, with Elucidations by Thomas Carlyle.* London: Methuen; 1904. Vol. 3, p. 101.

13  Quotations from the Instrument of Government, taken from Smith DL. *A History of the Modern British Isles, 1603–1707.* p. 185.

14  Coward B. *The Cromwellian Protectorate.* p. 17.

15  Roots I. (ed.). *Speeches of Oliver Cromwell.* London: Dent/Phoenix; 2002. p. 28–9.

16  Quoted in Smith DL. *A History of the Modern British Isles, 1603–1707.*

17  Smith DL. *A History of the Modern British Isles, 1603–1707.* p. 195.

18  Petition of the Gentlemen of Devon. In *Calendar of State Papers Domestic: Interregnum, 1659–60.* London: HMSO; 1886. p. 331.

19  Sir John Evelyn quoted in Smith DL. *A History of the Modern British Isles, 1603–1707.* p. 196.

20  Smith DL. *The Stuart Parliaments: 1603–1689.* p. 146.

21  Quoted in Scarboro D. *England 1625–1660: Charles I, the Civil War and Cromwell.* London: Hodder Education; 2005. p. 227.

22  Lomas SC. (ed.). *The Letters and Speeches of Oliver Cromwell, with Elucidations by Thomas Carlyle.* London: Methuen; 1904. Vol. 2, p. 108.

23  Carlyle T. *Oliver Cromwell's Letters and Speeches, With Elucidations.* Volume 3. Leipzig; 1861. p. 212.

# Glossary

**A**

**Artillery**   Part of the army. The term refers to the cannons and their crews that made up part of civil war armies. They were often large, cumbersome, slow to load and notoriously inaccurate.

**C**

**Cavalry**   Mounted soldiers used as the 'shock troops' of civil war armies. They were fast moving and were feared by unformed infantry. They were armed with swords, pistols, and musketoons (short muskets).

**Civil marriage**   A legal ceremony conducted by a representative of the state rather than by the Church.

**Coat and conduct money**   A prerogative tax that could be raised without parliamentary consent. In theory it paid for the provision and supply of the local militia.

**Coup d'état**   The act of overthrowing, or seizing control of government, through military force.

**I**

**Infantry**   Foot soldiers in the army, divided into 'Regiments of Foot'. Regiments were made up of musketeers and pikemen. While the musketeers provided the firepower, the pikemen provided the backbone to a formation in both defence and attack.

**O**

**Ordinance**   A law passed by Parliament without royal assent. Normally a Parliamentary Bill (a draft law) becomes an Act of Parliament (a law) only when it is signed by the monarch. During the civil war, Parliament was forced to use Ordinances instead in order to pass laws.

**R**

**Resolutions**   Often passed by Parliament or another political body, a Resolution would be passed by popular vote and would outline key policies or views.

**S**

**Shires**   Also known as 'counties', the shires were the local administrative unit of the Kingdom. The land-owning gentry of a county would return MPs to Parliament and every shire would have its own Lord Lieutenant (representative of the monarch), sheriff, Justices of the Peace and magistrates.

**T**

**Tyrannical**   Term used to describe the actions of a leader who exercised power in their own interests and to the detriment of their people.

# Acknowledgements

The authors and publishers acknowledge the following sources of copyright material and are grateful for the permissions granted. While every effort has been made, it has not always been possible to identify the sources of all the material used, or to trace all copyright holders. If any omissions are brought to our notice, we will be happy to include the appropriate acknowledgements on reprinting.

The publisher would like to thank the following for permission to reproduce their photographs:

**Chapter 1 opener:** Universal History Archive / Getty. Figure 1.1: Mary Evans Picture Library / Alamy Stock Photo. Figure 1.3: World History Archive / Alamy Stock Photo. Figure 1.4: Print Collector / Contributor/ Getty.
**Chapter 2 opener:** Mary Evans Picture Library / Alamy Stock Photo. Figure 2.1: Lodge Park and Sherborne Estate, Gloucestershire, UK / National Trust Photographic Library / Bridgeman Images. Figure 2.2: Classic Image / Alamy Stock Photo. Figure 2.3: Hulton Archive / Getty. Figure 2.4: British Library, London, UK / Bridgeman Images.
**Chapter 3 opener:** Houses of Parliament, Westminster, London, UK / Bridgeman Images. **Chapter 4 opener:** Cromwell Museum, Huntingdon, Cambridgeshire, UK. Figure 4.1: World History Archive / Alamy Stock Photo. Figure 4.2: Walker Art Gallery, National Museums Liverpool / Bridgeman Images. Figure 4.3: The Art Archive / Alamy Stock Photo. Figure 4.5: Pictorial Press Ltd / Alamy Stock. Figure 4.6: Private Collection / Bridgeman Images.
**Chapter 5 opener:** Print Collector / Getty Images. Figure 5.1: British Library Board. All Rights Reserved / Bridgeman Images. Figure 5.2: Private Collection / Bridgeman Images. Figure 5.3: Pictorial Press Ltd / Alamy Stock Photo.
**Chapter 6 opener:** Print Collector / Getty Images. Figure 6.2: Classic Image / Alamy Stock Photo. Figure 6.3: Look and Learn / Bridgeman Images

The publisher would like to thank the following for permission to reproduce extracts from their texts:

**Chapter 2 Extracts:** By permission of Harper Collins; Oxford University Press. **Chapter 3 Extract:** By permission of Orion Books.

# Index

Lightning Source UK Ltd.
Milton Keynes UK
UKOW07f1103080716

277863UK00009B/43/P